I0605883

HASTINGS

HASTINGS

A BOY'S OWN ADVENTURE

A memoir

DICK FRIZZELL

MASSEY UNIVERSITY PRESS

For Jude. Who's heard it all before.

CONTENTS

Introduction 8

1 Getting into it 13

2 Putting the map on Hastings 21

3 Shooting fish in a barrel 29

4 Rabbits for beer 35

5 The death of Stiffy Merton 41

6 They tried to tell us we're too young 49

7 Richard almost gets a brother 61

8 Flying a kite 67

9 Save the last dance for me 75

10 The Peak 81

11 Breaking the mould 89

12 Ban Irigham 97

13 First of six 103

14 I got a guts ache 111

15 Great balls of fire! 121

16 Mowing Molly's lawns 129
17 Tunnelling out of Hastings 139
18 Robinson's Dairy 151
19 The naked pie cart 163
20 That bastard boxthorn hedge 171
21 Cannery row 183
22 The Austin Ten-Four Sherborne 193
23 Younger than springtime 203
24 Ain't gonna work on McInnes's farm no more 211
25 The great park of Windsor 221
26 GJG 233
27 Fifth in line 247
28 Frankenstein is not the monster 257
29 Milkshakes with the devil 265
30 Where's the brick? 273

INTRODUCTION

How, or how not, to write a memoir? I'm slowly coming to the conclusion that there's no right way to do it. Are you going to dig deep and try to give a true account of yourself, or are you just going to tell a few entertaining yarns? I'm inclined to think that the former is bound to leak out of the latter if you can look past literary style and moral dissection and write as directly as possible. (I was going to say 'honestly' but I'm having an issue with that too.)

In fact I'm not even sure what my system is, apart from sitting there and remembering stuff and writing it down. A little memory, a little licence and a lot of humour. Like recalling the time, early in the morning, when the nightcart man and the milkman both arrived, clanking, at the gate at the same time and I lay there hoping they wouldn't bump into each other. Did it happen, or did I just make it up? I don't really care because it definitely *could* have happened.

I've jokingly said that it takes a lot of fiction to write non-fiction, but I think it's true. I lay out the frame of the story, which is without doubt inspired by actual events, and then my febrile imagination just flows into the gaps and creates the whole. The fiction, when it arrives, lands with such force that one can easily become convinced that the act of writing is bringing forth a forgotten truth. I love going down that corridor of detail: one detail piling onto another until the moment is done. Only then do I feel free to move on, searching for the next little seed of memory that I can build on.

I wrote 'Shooting fish in a barrel', the third yarn in this book, for a Radio New Zealand short story competition, only to be disqualified because I was, to my surprise, described as a 'published author'. But the damage was done: I was away.

All these stories cover those chaotic years when life starts to get complicated, when you become responsible for your own actions — when you dig a very long tunnel into a very unstable sawdust mountain, or flip your mother's car while hooning about down by the river, or catch your first glimpse of the awesome mysteries of pornography. I hope you get as much enjoyment from reading them as I did from writing them.

WELCOME
HASTINGS
THE FRUIT BOWL OF NEW ZEALAND

The author at three years old.

1

GETTING INTO IT

I was had. Funny to think of Mum 'having me' — at 9.15 a.m. on 11 August 1943, somewhere in the middle of the Second World War, in a nursing home in Mount Albert, Auckland.

Dad came ashore from his adventurous life in the Merchant Navy when they knew Mum was pregnant. He picked up a job with the Auckland Harbour Board, working on the dredges, which must have been a bit of a comedown after the insane anxieties of crewing in the engine rooms on those torpedo-dogged convoys sailing back and forth across the Pacific.

They rented a lovely sunny flat downstairs in a two-storeyed villa in Ponsonby's Picton Street. I must have been only about two years old but I have distinct memories of propelling my baby sister, Valerie, in her pram, perilously close to the edge of the verandah.

I suspect that the alarm bells this set ringing might have helped to burn the moment into my brain.

I also remember going upstairs with Mum to pay the rent to the owner, who looked like a caricature of a salty old sea captain, all white whiskers and turtle-neck sweater (though this could've been the beginning of me visualising my life in archetypes). He had worked as a wood grainer in the boat-building yards at Westhaven and his house was almost entirely and randomly wood-grained: walnut burr next to aspen, next to sycamore, next to oak, next to mahogany. Panel by panel.

And here's a story I don't remember, but one that Mum and Dad loved recounting. Every evening I used to toddle up to the gate to wait for Dad to come walking down Picton Street after getting off the tram on Ponsonby Road. One day he arrived, the gate was open and I wasn't there. In a panic my parents rushed up to the police station, which was only a couple of blocks away, and there I was, sitting up on the police sergeant's desk, bawling my eyes out, my little fists clutching overflowing handfuls of pennies. 'Thank God you're here,' they said. 'No amount of pennies will shut him up!'

The Frizzells' sunny sojourn on Picton Street only lasted a couple of years before Dad was lured down to the 'family seat' in Hastings, Hawke's Bay, by the offer of cheap mortgage financing from his two spinster sisters and a job as a shift engineer at the Tomoana Freezing Works. So, bye-bye Auckland and hello to the dynamic chaos of shift work.

He was in charge of maintaining the compressors that kept the ammonia surging through the pipes encircling the vast freezers full of export lamb. Because of the hands-on, hands-off irregularity of ammonia engineering, the workers were all housed, with their families if they had them, in a rough sort of village attached to the factory. The compressors that pumped the freezing liquid to every nook and corner of this massive complex were temperamental and so these men had to be right on hand to respond to any glitch in the highly lucrative trade in frozen lamb. The phone in the hall would ring in the middle of the night and I would hear Dad call out, 'Joan! Number three compressor's gone down!' and off he'd scoot, out the door and over the road into the plant that loomed up out of the stockyards and stoney acres of tobacco weed like Gormenghast, five stories of blackened concrete and rusty iron.

There was no kindergarten, no preschool, just little Richard out there in the wind, Mum back in the shack running the washing through the mangle and Dad over the road doing whatever he did with his giant machines. I seemed to have the run of the place. Whenever Mum sent me over to Dad's domain on some sort of a mission I'd make the most of it, wandering deeper and deeper into the complex of shunting yards, loading platforms and fat-rendering pits. I was fascinated by these great swimming-pool-sized ponds, rimmed with crusty edges of dirty yellow fat. The stench was astonishing.

Except for the locomotive driver who occasionally gave me a wave from way up in his cab, nobody seemed to take the slightest bit of notice of me. Sometimes I'd be passing a loading dock and a huge icy door would open with a great graunch and a group of shivering men would shuffle out blinking into the light, digging deep into their layers of wadded clothing for cigarettes and matches. Little did I know that one day I'd be joining the mole men in their subterranean employment.

In my usual solitary fog I'd follow the crisscrossing maze of railway lines until I reached the holding pens where the next day's flock stood quiet and still, oblivious to the fact that they were about to get an all-expenses-paid cruise to the Smithfield markets in London. On one occasion I kept walking, past the docile sheep and on to the notorious dormitories, where the seasonal workers from out of town bunked down for the duration. The din was terrific. Hooting and hollering: men playing Crown and Anchor, darning their socks, stitching up their sugar-bag jerkins, playing guitar. Everywhere there was laughing and joshing, especially around the Crown and Anchor game.

I remember the heady funk in the room, too: damp socks, the roast-mutton smell of their meals. The workers would take entire roast dinners over to the lunch canteen in Agee jars, heat them up in the oven and then plop it on a plate — something to supplement the hearts and sweetbreads they stripped from the sheep carcasses on the chain, shoved into mutton bags and boiled in the overhead steam vats used to hose down the butchered animals.

If I wasn't getting lost in the wonderland of stockyards and stink, I'd be exploring the hedges and paddocks around our house. One day I climbed a scrappy mānuka tree to feed the horse in the paddock next door. When I leant over with a handful of grass the branch I was on broke off at the trunk and down I went, only to be brought to an abrupt halt by another broken branch that penetrated my thigh and slid up under the skin between the bunched muscle fibres, leaving me strung up like a coat on a hook. I'm not sure how long I hung there squirming and screaming before Dad came down and unhooked me. I still have the scar.

It was quite a life. One night I was lying in bed with the sheets drawn up to my chin when Mum bustled past, holding a trap with a very large, very dead rat dangling from it. But the small neighbourhood did have an Ozarkian sort of charm, and a very hole-in-the-hedge fluidity. In fact Mum reckoned she saw the little girl next door show me her bottom through one of these handy vegetation breaks. I came into the kitchen to tell her that Kathleen had showed me her bottom, but I couldn't understand why she'd done it because I had one of my own.

Dad was a classic engineer. Everything was, in some way, engineering. He was constantly puzzled by 'art'. Why would you need art and design if you had engineering? Apparently engineering could solve anything.

One day the engineer decided to replace the rotting back steps with concrete slabs, which he decided he would move 'Egyptian style', using lengths of firewood as rollers. Mum was recruited to keep the chunks of concrete vertical while Dad provided the forward propulsion from the rear and I hopped around like a nuisance in my dressing gown and slippers.

It seemed to be a triumph of engineering, until Dad tried to position the slab towards its resting place and the logs refused to behave. One by one they spun out from under the bottom edge, Dad lost the vertical balance, and God knows how many pounds of concrete slowly toppled to one side and onto me and Mum.

You'll have to imagine the ruckus because I don't remember a thing from that point on. Dad managed to lever the slab up enough to get Mum's legs — minus a shoe — out and then I evidently just slid out like a slice of tomato from a ham sandwich with only a nasty gash on my knee.

How was I still alive? Apparently Mum's sensible shoe had wedged sideways under the slab and had taken all the weight. Given the physics of the shoe-fulcrum and the obvious fact of my survival I can only assume this to be true.

And then there was the cart that engineer Dad decided to engineer. Now, a typical cart is a skeletal thing like a big capital letter 'I', one central bar with two cross bars and a pram wheel at each extremity. The front cross bar pivots for steering and the rider controls the steering rope from the three-sided beer crate mounted amidships. We can all picture it.

But God put engineers on this earth to make things better, and so Dad went all-out to build a better cart. For a start he decided on a wheelbase twice as long as the norm, with a connecting board as wide as a scaffolding plank. The cross bars were replaced with axles — actual axles — and somewhere he'd found a crate, or box, big enough that when it was stood on end I could sit in it as if it were a sentry box, or cab. In front of the box, where my legs extended, he fashioned a long, hooped cowling, which bore a passing resemblance to an old-fashioned truck bonnet. He painted the whole thing barn red.

The crowning touch was the steering mechanism. No ropes and feet for this pantechnicon: Dad's skills had gone into hyper-drive. Even at the tender age of four I knew this arrangement was special. I sat in the cab in front of a bona-fide steering wheel mounted on a shaft that passed through a passable looking dashboard all the way down through the bonnet to a spectacular mechanism called a 'crown and pinion', two of Dad's favourite words. This fabulous device looked like two conical gears engaged at cross purposes, thus enabling me to steer the thing from my imperious position in the cab.

Dad couldn't get an engine under the bonnet with both of my legs in there, so he supplied the motive power by pushing the rear end of the flat-bed with a long-handled garden hoe, which meant he could run alongside in regal style in his baggy ex-military khaki shorts without doing that awkward bending-over-pushing thing. It was a magnificent piece of engineering.

The house at the Tomoana works was also the site of my first encounter with paint. When Dad took it upon himself to paint the roof of our rented white-weatherboard box he decided that I should witness the process. So up the ladder I went. Almost immediately I slipped on a wet patch and continued on my back, down the gentle slope, grabbing the tin of paint and bringing it with me until I finally lodged myself in the guttering. I hung there grimly at the edge of the roof as the paint ran down the corrugations, spilling over and around me before cascading to the ground below. Somehow or other Dad managed to fish me out and carry me into the washhouse, where he scrubbed me from head to toe with turpentine. There was green paint in my navel for years.

Dad must have been promoted from shift engineer to regular engineer or some such because we left Okefenokee for the relatively civilised pebble-dash suburbia (if suburbia can be eight blocks away from the CBD) of Hastings Street, Hastings. Then Dad got the promised low-interest loan and we moved down a few blocks to 507 Sylvan Road, a big, turreted villa where the Frizzells set up house for the next 35 or so years. I moved from Hastings Central to Parkvale Primary, over by my beloved Windsor Park, and it was in this part of town that the following tales slowly unfolded.

The Hastings clock tower.

2

PUTTING THE MAP ON HASTINGS

But first, a pause for a bit of geography and history. Where were we? Where was Hastings? Why was it so close to Napier and why was that little place halfway between called Clive? What a strange line-up — Hastings, Napier, Clive — it sounded like a clarion call from one of my *Boy's Own Paper* cavalry charges. I think I honestly didn't know the difference between a Māori place name and a Pākehā one. I think I thought Bridge Pā and Taradale were Māori names and Te Mata Peak and Tomoana (T'mona) were English.

Historians hadn't found us yet. We had no right to exist. We were just there, all thrown together on the Heretaunga (English?) Plains like survivors in some sort of lost magic kingdom of rivers and stopbanks — miles and miles of stopbanks — built by a lost civilisation. Driving out and driving in were considered epic journeys. Auckland might have been on another planet.

None of this bothered me; if I'd been asked to vote on it I would've said I'd landed at the centre of the universe. Standing on our corner of Sylvan Road and Victoria Street, with Te Mata Peak, the Tukituki River and the mad wilderness of Windsor Park to the back of me and the distinctly non-wilderness of Cornwall Park and the misty vista of the Ruahines in front of me, I was the master of all I could barely survey. A few blocks to the left of me the one main road ran directly up to the mighty Hastings CBD: three cinemas, a Woolworths *and* our own Westerman's — a real department store, complete with money-sucking vacuum tubes. Could you ask for more?

Well, you could ask for a library, and there it was, up at my end of town. Set in a row of official-looking civic spaces flowing up Heretaunga Street from the big Spanish-style town hall, it sat back behind some very imposing doors in a huge gloomy brown space set about with large glass cases containing models of famous ocean liners, each about the size of a kitchen bench. Some were split down the middle and displayed against a mirror that gave the illusion of a whole vessel. Others you could walk right around and peer into the portholes or right into the bridge and out the other side.

Books and boats, what a romantic association. You had to turn your back on this labyrinth of vitrines to contemplate the books, of which there was a head-spinning selection: all the *Biggles* books, the *Just William* series and a complete collection of Westerns about some young cowboy who lived with his golden palomino in the exotic dreamland of Colorado.

Right down the seriously gloomy end of this small-town

Bodleian I found a selection of very dark books about the Second World War. I don't know how they got there, or how I discovered them, but I'll never forget pulling one of them down and opening it to a shocking photo essay of the day the Americans cautiously moved into the concentration camps. Such horrors a young boy should never have seen, but I saw them and even ducked back for another look every time I went in for the latest Willard Price adventure. Feeling somehow guilty, I never shared my discovery with anyone.

In my third-form year — when I was about 12 or 13 — the library moved over to a bright new war memorial building with a specially commissioned Peter McIntyre mural; the ships and the dark books didn't make it across. Too much darkness for this overlit horror of a book repository. I hated the place, but I loved the mural.

I'm not going to walk you all the way down Heretaunga Street — it took me long enough to get around the library — but suffice it to say it was, still is, an impressively lengthy thoroughfare. The actual road, skipping along under several different aliases, runs south to north all the way from Havelock North to Fernhill. The railway line runs east–west, bisecting it at a right angle, and what was then a smart little gridded agri-service town clustered around the junction. It looked like a crucifix laid out on a patchwork quilt, with Christ's feet resting on the southernmost 30 mph sign and Aunty Molly's frock shop and the railway station right there in His left armpit. Actually, if you want to extend this daft simile, the gasworks would be in the Saviour's right armpit and His head would sit under the halo of the Stortford Lodge roundabout.

We lived a block inside that southern speed limit marker. Dad's brother George, a tall, quiet — apart from his wheezing asthmatic chest — market gardener with a heavily weathered face, lived directly opposite us on the more rural, northern edge of town. Aunty Molly, with her tidy house and garden, lived pretty much smack-dab in the middle. Aunty Nora, the brisk and literate ex-schoolteacher, lived over on the east coast at Bay View, where her beachfront cottage did indeed have a view of the bay, with an even closer view from the tripod telescope upstairs in the sunroom.

You could've ridden your bike around Hastings before lunch. My primary school was a short walk south and the thriving commercial hub of Robinson's Corner — the dairy, grocery, butcher, chemist and fish and chip shop — was only a couple of blocks north. All our material needs catered for within a three-block radius. No wonder I felt a bit special.

We were surrounded by orchards and there was a sawmill. Has there ever been a better playground? Always something to eat, somewhere to build, shoot or hide away in. Always something to nearly get killed by.

After we moved in to 507 Sylvan road, the rest of the sisters duly arrived — and a brother, eventually. The house filled up. Did Mum always know she was going to need a house this big? My little bedroom at the kitchen end of the hall became a sacred place — no sisters allowed — home to apple boxes full of *Phantom* and *Uncle Scrooge* comics.

Hastings filled up as well. In the mid-1950s, and without any noticeable difference in infrastructure or personality, it became a city. By then it already had its world-famous Blossom Festival with its highlight parade of floats. Oh, how we loved that parade. Clubs, groups, shops and expressive individuals spent days, weeks, months, preparing for it.

A group of self-important citizens who had formed Greater Hastings later turned their attention to a vast and impossible project: New Zealand's Disneyland in Windsor Park. They called it Fantasyland, and they nearly pulled it off. Using volunteer labour, cheap cement and limited design skills, they cobbled together a pretty impressive cluster of quite sizeable things. There was a fairytale castle you could actually almost get lost in, a pirate ship as big as an Elizabethan galleon sitting in a large kerbed puddle, a concrete shoe for the old woman to live in and a miniature railway designed to wend its chuffing way through cunning overpasses and underpasses and past Humpty Dumpty on his wall and the space rocket assembled from what looked suspiciously like plumbing supplies.

Time, children and weather weren't kind to Fantasyland and the civic riches many thought it would generate never eventuated. It seemed to slip from a vision of future possibilities to a ghost town in about a decade. Eventually it was rebuilt as a waterslide complex called Splash Planet. But I was well gone by then.

The Blossom Festival, too, suffered a few setbacks. In 1960 railcar loads of rampaging hoons up from the infamous Hutt Valley ripped its rosy reputation to bits, and the man of vision and head of PR for the Greater Hastings committee absconded to Australia with the festival funds and the festival secretary.

But never mind, we still had the Hastings Highland Games,

when the whole town went Scottish for a month: bagpipers practising in backyards, the keening whine drifting off on the early evening air; marching girls rubbing fake tan into their sturdy Kiwi legs; highland dancers polishing their brooches. All that was happening just around the corner from me in my dear old Windsor Park, where you could rent a canoe or watch a few red-faced, bandy-legged giants toss a caber about the arena.

Writ large on a great billboard on the edge of town was the most enduring symbol of our success: 'The Fruit Bowl of New Zealand'. That's what we were. It could've been 'The Meat Pack of New Zealand' too, if they'd pushed it. Blossoms and lambs featured together on postcards. We'd go on Sunday drives to look at them, the lambs gambolling in the foothills of the Ruahines and the blossom pretty much everywhere you looked.

I don't remember driving out to see the pea blossom but there must have been acres of it. If you weren't inside Wattie's looking at peas, you were out in the fields harvesting them.

Somehow this gormless little dreamer bumped happily along on this wave of vaguely delusional rural enthusiasm, hiding in the art room at school or tucked away in his gloomy bedroom at 507 copying out his favourite comic panels and pinning the results to the wall. I drifted through my schooling doing the barest minimum of what was required. I did Standard Four twice when it was discovered that I'd somehow got a year ahead. It didn't bother me — I wasn't in a hurry. School seemed OK, never felt like a burden. I'd walk off in the morning, then walk home mid-afternoon with what felt like the whole day ahead of me.

There was time enough to bike around to Billy Fulton's and play with his two-way radio or dig out an extension to the underground hut. There were infinitely long summer evenings with that occasional weird light at dusk that made the few flowers that survived Dad's gardening glow like torches. And freezing winter mornings that exploded the milk bottles full of water that we put out at night on the tank stand.

It was a life of constant excitement.

The author's Strangely Normal shirt.

3

SHOOTING FISH IN A BARREL

It was Leo's idea; the maddest ones always were. He'd heard his father say it: 'It was like shooting fish in a barrel!' Leo loved the sound of this. 'It means that whatever it is, it should be easy. Geddit?' He thought we should give it a go, and we decided to go along with it — give it a shot, so to speak. We had nothing else on. We never did.

The barrel was easy. Leo's dad had rigged one up at the end of a downpipe around the back of the packing shed where we would take turns dunking ourselves on those hot Hawke's Bay summer days.

Guns weren't much of a problem either. Most of us had air rifles or pistols of varying descriptions: I had a very peculiar-looking handgun that featured, above the butt and the trigger, a pencil-thin barrel mounted above a thing that resembled a short bicycle pump. The thin barrel was the lever that pumped the propulsive air into the big barrel while at the same time acting as the actual tube that sent the slug on its busy way. All up, a very unweapon-like apparatus and I was always a bit coy about displaying it.

We used this motley armoury to play a dangerous sort of Cowboys and Indians where we loaded our guns with limestone grit. We just poured it down the barrel and blasted away at each other in quite spectacular fashion from various forms of concealment. If you managed to sneak up on an unsuspecting buttock you could inflict quite an impressive wound that looked oddly like a large ringworm lesion. Something to do with the rifling in the barrel, I suspect. Thank God we were smart enough not to shoot at each other with actual slugs, those little lead wheatsheaf-shaped projectiles that wreaked havoc on the bird, apple and tin can numbers in the neighbourhood.

Fish, though, were a problem. Where the hell do you get live fish? Decent, shootable-sized fish? The goggle-eyed cockabullies we more or less sieved out of the local streams and creeks weren't going to do it. Some bright spark said he'd heard that you could catch plenty of decent fish off the sewage outlet along a particularly bleak stretch of local foreshore, but that was too much palaver. This was a science experiment, not a fishing expedition. At Simon's suggestion, we trooped off to the town's one and only pet store to look at the goldfish. Not much of a target really. Not much better than cockabullies.

Then Gavin remembered the lily ponds in the big park at the flash end of town. Some big goldfish in there, apparently. So now we were starting to really organise ourselves: bikes, buckets and a trout net, thanks once again to Leo's dad's shed.

Under the cover of dark, and a movie-going alibi, we cycled up to the park, me giving Leo a double, with bucket and net balanced on the handle bars. It proved to be a remarkably straightforward exercise. We sneaked up to the pond's edge of decoratively laid rocks and just started blindly thrusting the trout net into the lily pads.

We netted one healthy specimen almost immediately, just as one of the high school prefects strode by with his girlfriend in tow. Footsteps crunching on the gravel, us crouching in the damp grass like black toads in the moonlight. The second fish took a bit longer, long enough to convince us that two was enough. Two was plural. We upended the second fish into the bucket and wobbled off into the night. I stowed the bucket in the woodshed, behind the mealy old firewood at the back where I kept my cigarette papers and matches.

A couple of days later we got the fish into the barrel. Well, we got one fish into the barrel; the other one was dead when I retrieved the bucket from its hiding place. Maybe the crushed-up Snax biscuits didn't suffice. Could've been the salt.

So now we had a fish in a barrel and were beginning to feel a bit half-hearted about the whole exercise. The actual logistics were starting to look a bit daunting too. Just how do you shoot a rifle into a barrel? We were going to have to stand on boxes. Maybe it was meant to be 'shooting fish in a half-barrel'.

As we stood in a despondent arc, Leo came striding around the corner of the packing shed with a real gun, a .303. Beside our air rifles it looked like an elephant gun. He'd crept into his mum and dad's bedroom while they were both out and unclipped the gun from its proud display above the fireplace.

He wordlessly passed me the gun while he clambered up onto the apple boxes. Then, to our amazement, he kept on climbing until he was standing on the rim of the barrel with his bare feet planted just so, his back pressed up against the downpipe and his eyes fixed on the rippling surface of the water. He gestured towards me and I passed him the rifle hand over hand before retreating to the shelter of the nearest macrocarpa. Out of the corner of my eye I noticed Gavin and Simon also taking a few judicious steps backwards.

Was the thing even loaded? Was it cocked? Ready to go? Had Leo ever fired a .303 before?

I couldn't believe he'd do it. But he did.

Standing oddly poised, with the great weapon pointing down between his feet into the big oak barrel, he pulled the trigger.

Leo bounced back sideways off the drainpipe and the gun fell into the water as he slid and crashed from the barrel, to the boxes, and onto the ground. The sound of the shot echoed off across the plains, gradually fading as Leo's yelps of pain rose to replace it.

Gavin, quiet and steady Gavin, climbed in and hauled out the rifle, assisted in the process by the fact that the water level was rapidly receding. The bullet had, of course, gone through the barrel, taking a significant portion of a stave with it. Its trajectory must have been deflected by the shallow angle at which it struck the resilient oak, chewing its way downwards, carving out a deepening groove before being deflected and exiting just above the lowest iron hoop. The water fountained out of the gash in a long rooster-tailed plume until the frantic carp lodged itself in the gap like a frankfurter lying in an American hot dog bun.

Gavin, unruffled and motionless in the barrel, crouched down and extricated the sad fish from the shambles and handed it to me. I transferred it back to the bucket. Leo lay sideways on the limestone, pedalling himself wildly in a mad scrabbling circle while clutching his collarbone, undoubtedly broken by the savage kick-back of the mighty .303.

Gavin had the gun, I had the fish, Leo had his collarbone and Simon had his mouth open as we all waited for the world to collapse around us. Nothing happened. I guess the shot could have sounded like another farmer having a go at his magpies, and boys break bones falling out of apple trees every day of the week.

We helped Leo back into the house and clipped the drying rifle back into its wall mount. I cycled home, topped up the bucket and put it back in the woodshed. Later in the evening I took the fish back to the park and tipped it, still alive, back into the lily pond.

Gavin dug the bullet out of the ground, took it to school and, in metalwork, polished it up, drilled a hole in it and wore it round his neck on a string. Leo recovered. His dad plugged the hole in the barrel, said it looked like someone had been inside it trying to chop their way out with an axe. Of course Leo had no idea what he was talking about. The gun was still clipped to the bedroom wall. Leo's dad hadn't been out hunting yet. I hope he has a good look down the barrel before he does.

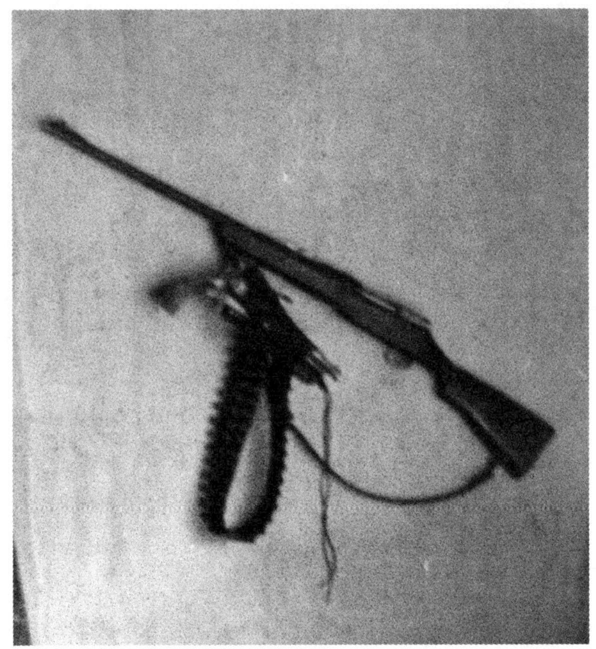

The author's father's .303.

4

RABBITS FOR BEER

My father was a strange man. I could never rationalise the wild screwy-eyed drunk alone at the kitchen table at the end of the day with the demure and self-effacing gentleman setting off for work at the beginning of it.

He was the classic functioning alcoholic, even loudly claiming on one occasion — at the end of the day — that he wasn't an alcoholic at all, but a drunkard, and that he could give it up any time he liked. And he would. He'd stop drinking for two or three days and then, having proved his point, wallop back into it.

He was brought up by his mother and two spinster sisters in rural Hawke's Bay, his farming father having died in a mysterious shotgun incident. Suicide was never mentioned, but the circumstances were hinted at. Losing one farm in Dannevirke to a

Māori leasehold loophole and losing heart at the grind of starting another one over in Feilding, he solved all his problems one grim afternoon, alone down in the cowshed. But it wasn't suicide: he was just putting the gun down in the corner, placing the butt on the concrete.

Dad was a bit of a golden boy: dux of his high school — he was quite a reader, always pushing strange and exotic authors, such as Rafael Sabatini, Daniel Defoe and Alexandre Dumas, my way — smart engineering apprentice, dashing marine engineer in the wartime Pacific. (I often wondered how much the move from Auckland to Hawke's Bay rankled.) At the freezing works he quickly rose to become chief engineer of the engine room. He never got to be *chief* engineer of the whole shooting box, and I think that rankled a bit too.

But his job was a responsible one and he took it very seriously. He was a responsible man. The tight and boxy engineer's script he used to log every day's input and output attested to that — the same crisp capitals that he used in his cryptic crossword puzzles. Crisp, crisp, everything just so. The hooter at the works blasting on the dot every day without fail. His wristwatch propped up on the Möbius loop of its expanding metal strap, next to his plate where he could keep an eye on it as he ate his tidy lunch, meat and vegetables on separate plates. Where do you pick up an affectation like that? So fussy, so quietly prim. The soft and sibilant 'How do you do?' on the big black telephone whenever he answered it. The white overalls he slipped into at work out the back of the office with its tidy ledgers. The collar turned up like a tennis coach, the top button undone to show collar and tie. Shiny brown shoes, not boots; the workers wore boots.

And then, at 7 p.m. or so, after 6 o'clock closing and a snort or two at the 'club', in rolled this crazy drunk. Dinner in the coal range oven, plate covered with a plate, but no separation of the victuals for this version of Dick Frizzell Snr. Not lurching angry drunk but 'I'm not pissed and I can enunciate everything with perfect precision' drunk. And ridiculously argumentative. I once picked up his special industrial-strength torch, which he'd laid on the kitchen table. It was the one he wore jauntily, if you can do that with a torch, in the hip pocket of those white overalls, the one he used to shine a light on all the pressure valves and dials in the dank dungeons of the freezers.

For insulation, and protection, this impressive tool was encased entirely in black rubber. You had to press a designated spot on the outer sleeve to activate the actual button beneath. I liked the slightly remote and fluttery sensation of pressing through the latex to the metal.

Anyway, drunk Dad grabbed it out of my hand, held it aloft, loudly announced, 'This torch is *indestructible*!' and hurled it with all his might at the kitchen wall, where it exploded into a cloud of glass, bulbs, batteries and rubber. I looked back at Dad, who was staring in shock and horror at the wall as if it had somehow let him down. I suddenly remembered that I had homework to do.

Teach by example. And never compliment anyone on a job well done or they'd get a swollen head, apparently, and stop trying. Watch and learn seemed to be the principle. Watch me plant these potatoes, watch me check the tyre pressure with this shiny little pop-out gizmo. Watch me skin this rabbit, after you've watched me sharpen this evil-looking butcher's knife. Watch me down this large brown bottle of beer before I do either. God, the beer! Beer and hunting. Sharp knives, rifles and beer.

He used to take me with him on 'educative' expeditions, up into the back hills of a friend's farm in the wild Ruahines. He'd start out with his baggy old canvas rabbit bag full of those large brown bottles and the ratio of rabbits to bottles would slowly change in the course of the day as the animals got shot and the empty soldiers were left behind in gullies and rabbit holes.

And, of course, I experienced all this in real time. Watching and learning as the quiet and reserved father at the wheel on the way up turned into a crazy careening lunatic on the way down. He would freewheel the old Austin all the way from the mountains to the foothills, cutting corners with wild abandon, all the while loudly singing 'Hava Nagila'. Were we Jewish? Where did that come from? I still wonder. I never knew whether to be panicked or proud of this mad performance. Were we going to die? How much beer can a man drink and still drive?

Skinning and gutting a rabbit. One quick cut around each foot, one around the anus somehow, and then with his boot planted on the back legs he'd magically turn the rabbit inside out with one wet, continuous rip. The exposed neck was sliced through and head and skin were discarded in the grass, soon to be followed, after another quick flick of the knife, by guts, heart, lungs, etc. Early on in the trip, while there were more bottles of beer than rabbits in the bag, he'd point out to me things like the peristaltic turd marbles in the lower intestine and how far you had to scrabble around up in the chest cavity to get all the 'small bits'.

But as the ratio of bottle to rabbit shifted he'd get more and more primal until he'd be standing there lurching about with his big old dad-penis out as he pissed like a horse into the steaming puddle of guts and skin. I'm surprised he didn't throw his head back and howl. Blood would seep through the bag and down the back of his windbreaker as we trudged quietly back to the car, then made our way off into the rural twilight, the old car bumping over the farm tracks, long grass brushing the drive shaft until we got to the gravel. With a boot full of rabbits and a father full as a boot, winding up for a bit of folk singing, we would scoot down towards the twinkling lights of Hawke's Bay and home.

Stiffy Merton on his motorbike.
The author is in the sidecar.

5

THE DEATH OF STIFFY MERTON

Dad had a large roster of mates of whom Mum, for some reason or another, didn't approve. And Mum had her 'nice' friends who Dad politely put up with. Actually, Dad was such a compliant person that as long as he had a whisky handy I don't think he really cared who was sitting on the other side of the card table. But he did love the loose group of unruly mavericks that he hung onto. Maybe it was those years in the Merchant Navy that bred that sort of male kinship; they definitely were the business.

The one who fascinated me most was a mysterious uncle or cousin of Dad's who worked as a shepherd at the freezing works. Tim lived alone in one of a short row of small dark cribs, each with its lonely 'shade' tree growing out of the puggy mud, lined up next to the sheep-shitty corrals, on the side of the works where all the animals were delivered and penned. The colour-blind loco driver lived next door: he just knew that the top light meant stop.

It was 1955 but Tim looked as if he'd just come back from the war and still hadn't unpacked. Such dark and spartan digs. A biscuit tin on the table next to an open butter pack and his rollies. Bare boards on the tiny porch and yellowed newspapers pasted over the match-lining. It all felt like the cowboy books I loved reading.

My enthusiasm for his gloomy circumstances must have impressed Uncle Tim because one day he dug an old leather money belt out from one of his trunks and prised a gold sovereign from inside the worn lining, shook it out into the palm of his hand and handed it to me with a grunt and a 'Here you go, Richard'. I lost it years ago, of course, but it's a powerful memory.

If Tim was the spookiest of Dad's private circle, then the wackiest and definitely the sunniest were Mona and Keith Ingram. 'Rough as sacks', Mum called them — and sacking did seem to be a bit of a theme. Keith had set up their garage as a serious party place. Down at ground level, well below the trusses and skylights, all available wall space was taken up by mismatched couches and armchairs, camp stools, beer fridges, a bar and a stereo. At eye level were the decorations: artificial flowers and NAC posters. But the thing that got me the first time I saw it and made me love the place was the large sack with a big red heart painted in the centre and the message 'Keith Loves Mona' scrawled in black within its borders that hung high above the general décor.

How could that be? Grown-up people in love and more or less partying on the footpath every Sunday afternoon sure as hell wasn't my experience. Mum and Dad were affectionate enough but I'd never seen a public declaration like this before. I'd sit in the corner on a box with sacking upholstery and marvel at the whole scene. Shouts and cheers, glasses raised, as Nat King Cole crooned away on the stereo and passers-by stuck their heads in and made loud jokes about the suffering of 'the other half'.

Dad would sit there with a beer and a fag, happy smile on his face, taking it easy and always well fit to drive home. Mum *never* went to Sunday drinks in the garage. She might have been to art school but she was no bohemian. Well, maybe a little, with her skiffle bands and her drama groups, but declarations of love in a garage? No way.

Now there was one friend Mum almost approved of — Gentleman Jack Porter — but though he came close, he still didn't qualify for Mum's inner circle. (Pity he didn't play the guitar or the piano accordion.) None of this seemed to bother Jack. He'd turn up for a Sunday drink on the porch and tease Mum a bit: 'What are you up to in there, Joan? You burning those biscuits again?'

I simply adored Jack. He was well over six feet tall, with long arms, hands like hams and a voice from the bottom of a well. Jack lived in a dark house down the road with an agoraphobic blind son — no wife. He was, I think, a bit of a man of letters, which probably made Mum nervous and attracted Dad. He taught me a bunch of poems whose original words were swapped out for fruity synonyms and florid embellishments. For example, instead of 'This is the house that Jack built', he would intone, 'This is the domiciliary edifice erected by Jack' or 'This is the fermented commodity deposited in the . . .' or 'This is the rodent of predatory instincts who devoured the . . .'

I memorised the whole thing right up to 'This is the bovine ruminant with a corrugated frontal appendage of osseous excretion who . . .' I could never quite grasp the rest about the milkmaid and the vicar. It was quite a party trick. I loved that booming voice giving Dad and me personal recitals: 'Scintillate, scintillate, gaseous orb.' It's a pity Mum never got the hang of Jack. I learnt all he had to give, over a dark table in a dark house.

The king of Dad's dodgy mates was an extraordinary character called Stiffy Merton. Where to start with Stiffy? Extremely tall and rangy, he looked a lot like Edmund Hillary — jutting jaw, curly forelock, always grinning. He owned a vast barn full of mechanical parts, a bit like the places that the boys keep finding on the TV show *American Pickers*. But, unlike them, his main emphasis was on Harley Davidson motorbikes and all the gear that went with them: the flying helmets, goggles, gloves. I loved that barn. It never seemed to end. One day I found an old, worn pair of brown leather boxing gloves and Stiffy let me keep them. I made a punching bag out of one of Dad's Navy duffle bags, stuffed it tight with walnut tree leaves, hung it from one of the lower 'chin-up' branches and whaled away at it like Rocky Graziano.

I've got a press photo from one of the Hastings Blossom parades of me sitting up the front of a sidecar hooked up to one of Stiffy's Indians. I've only got a dim memory of this bit of grandstanding, but there I am, looking straight ahead, grinning like Stiffy Merton, proud in his greatcoat, with my little blond quiff curling back in the slipstream. I'm not sure if Stiffy ever got to see the photo because not long after that, he left us.

Dad, Stiffy and Jack Porter would sometimes take their big guns, the .303s, and hike high up into the Ruahines to hunt for pigs or deer. (Definitely not rabbits. This was real man stuff.) Off they'd go in the Austin, loaded up with bivouac material, billies, pans and no doubt some whisky.

On this occasion, the three of them took off on the second day from their base on a long ridge just below the snow line. Somewhere along the way Stiffy sat down on a log to catch his breath and have a smoke. Said he'd catch them up later. After a spell they got a bit concerned, retraced their footsteps and found Stiffy on the ground by the log, still in the seated position, but stiff as a board.

They couldn't carry him out, not a big bloke like that, so they hiked back, got in the Austin and drove down for help. Eventually they found a bloke at the Mareakakaho marae who drove back up behind them with a horse in a trailer, and they brought the body out on horseback. Dad said Stiffy was in the perfect staple shape to get him over the back of the horse.

With a bit of trial and error they got him back to the Austin and, yes, Stiffy was still in the perfect position to be sat up in the passenger seat. Jack Porter went back down with the owner of the horse and Dad drove his dead friend back to town. He said it was a bloody nightmare, Stiffy rocking back and forth in the seat and side to side on the corners — no seat belts back then — and occasionally giving out odd farts and grunts as the car bounced over rocks or ridges in the road. Internal gas build-up, according to Dad. It was night by then and there was Dad squinting over the wheel, imagining his passenger coming back to life, and nudging him back to vertical as he lurched about.

Dad never went hunting again — not for the big stuff anyway.

Stiffy's death and the ghastly aftermath knocked him around. Not long after that I found him sitting on the side of his bed crying — not drunk crying, too early in the day for that — and he said to me, 'All my friends are dying.' Maybe old Uncle Tim had gone too, and who knows who else from Dad's previous life, but Keith and Mona and Jack Porter were still there, and all of Mum's approved friends.

The Castle Films logo, circa 1950.

6

THEY TRIED TO TELL US WE'RE TOO YOUNG

Who goes camping a stone's throw from where they live? Well, half of Hastings it would appear. No one seemed to think that there was anything unusual about it: get everyone you hang out with in town to pitch their tents cheek by jowl in a camping ground so close to home that Dad could still go into work each day and be back in time to fire up the Coleman cooker so Mum could fry up our share of the day's catch.

Our merry little gathering of the proletariat was out at the fabulously basic Te Awanga camping ground. Basic in a good way, I should say, or basic in the only way anything could be back in 1955. Anything you'd expect to find in a camping ground was there, all the amenities, though I suspect they'd be laughable by today's standards. But we loved it. Those flash tents with multiple rooms, atriums and complicated zips hadn't been invented and everyone seemed to be sourcing their equipment from army surplus supplies. Just the standard square 'room' with hefty centre pole, roll-up tabs, guy ropes and tent pegs. Ropes everywhere, all draped with wet togs and towels.

Most of these heavy canvas tents had a caravan attached. The ubiquitous Liteweight, which sat there on its site waiting for summer. Like a cabin, really, on wheels — or what used to be wheels and were now blocks of wood. I loved that the tent floor (i.e. the paddock) was quite a bit lower than the floor of the caravan. You had to go up and in to get from the almost-not-there contained space of the tent to the most-definitely-there intimate space of the caravan. Lying on your camp stretcher in the tent was like lying out in the open compared with stretching out on Mum and Dad's big bed at the rear of the caravan.

All the cooking and food prep was done in the tent as well. I can't remember Mum ever using the kitchen, such as it was, in the caravan. This was the fabulous thing about camping: the casual egalitarian air of all the usual protocols, guy ropes crisscrossing and boundaries blurred. Am I eating Mum's fried fish, or Mrs McLeay's?

All washing was done, of course, in the ablution block, an echoey concrete bunker of a thing built bald and unmissable right in the middle of the grounds. It was a weird place — the water on the floors, the random soap shards on the hand basins, the soft waves of chatter and clatter. All the domestic stuff you'd never dream of sharing at home — teeth brushing, hair combing, toilet flushing — all up there side by side in a row. There was not a lot of need for showering because we swam all day, but there was always a sleepy adult or two, friends of your parents you usually knew quite formally, heading for the stalls in their dressing gowns and slippers, cradling the classic sponge bag, flannel and towel close to their chest.

I don't think the concept of barbecuing had arrived in New Zealand back then. Not in Hawke's Bay anyway. Everyone seemed to rely solely on the faithful Coleman: you could hear them being pumped as you walked between the tents.

We ate a lot of processed meat and salad. You know, iceberg lettuce — just called lettuce back then — with homemade condensed milk mayonnaise and Wattie's beetroot. We ate in our damp togs on our towels on our camp stretchers, while the grown-ups, nearly always in groups of three or more, ate sitting about in those canvas chairs, the ones that collapsed together when you picked them up. Probably army surplus too.

There was always a fold-out table by the centre pole that was covered in packets of tea, biscuits, salt and pepper. A box of apples might be sitting beneath. Above the table, various bags, bottle openers and tea towels hung on nails driven straight into the pole. Serious stuff such as flour and so on was stored in the caravan kitchen cupboards but everything else was stacked and propped around the inside perimeter of the tent, and the outside. Some tents had chests of drawers and God knows what other furniture up against the sagging canvas, which always seemed a bit bizarre. Weren't we out here to *not* do that?

How did the provisioning thing work? Did Dad bring fresh stuff back with him from work, or was it Wattie's all the way? Probably Wattie's, though I seem to remember a produce truck doing the rounds of the camping grounds. We ate a lot of fish, I know that.

There was another camping ground just a few miles up the road and around the coast, sitting in the crook of Cape Kidnappers like the reel on a fishing rod. This rival establishment was called Clifton, which, in my overwrought imagination, meant the beginnings of the cape's cliffs, which loomed above it, but was more likely named after the first doughty fellow to launch his fishing boat off its gravelly shore, old Clifton Gordon. This was Clifton's main function: the boat launching. There was no way you could launch a boat at Te Awanga with its lagoon bar and surf break, so all the fishing dads kept their boats at Clifton.

This lofty function conferred a curious sort of clubby air on the camping ground. You went in past the gatehouse/shop with all its posted rules and regulations as if you were entering another country. Even the tents and caravans seemed somehow more special, perhaps because everyone was in the one 'street' that ran along the foot of the cliffs, more gentle and bush-clad than the looming monsters further around. Our place, Te Awanga, had a chaotic air that made it very hard to discern the organising principle behind the layout of the sites. Clifton was more ordered, more bossy. And, of course, it had *the ramp*. You went there to use the ramp. Did you pay? I don't know, but an air of officialdom always hung over the proceedings.

Our main man and regular campsite neighbour was Bill Winchester. He was one of those long and lanky, large-handed types who handled all things mechanical and mysterious with impressively casual panache. And his boat was a whopper, like those whaling boats that Moby Dick liked to reduce to matchwood with his jaws and tail, one long clinker-built open hull with a massive diesel engine sitting squarely amidships. I seem to remember the seating running right around the edges a couple of feet below the gunwales with only a couple of conventional crossway benches fore and aft.

Bill had two warnings before launching: 'Don't touch the exhaust' and 'Stay clear of the drive shaft'. Can you imagine? This great, beamy thing like a Viking longboat full of kids fired up with excitement and expectation, leaping and clambering around a fully exposed eight-cylinder truck engine at full throttle. But Bill knew what he was doing. One of the several tractors on hand would get the great thing down the ramp and we'd all jump aboard — kids, adults and bystanders — and out we'd go. How anyone caught anything I have no idea. I was nine or ten, what did I care? I loved luncheon sausage and, besides, I was too busy picturing myself wrapped around that drive shaft. But catch plenty they always did. We all ate fish, again, that night back at Te Awanga.

The Winchesters were an interesting lot. They were Catholics, which meant, for reasons I never really understood, that we didn't see a lot of them back in town, but somehow it didn't seem to matter out there under the canvas. Bill was a bit of a Stiffy Merton, didn't say much except a gruff, 'G'day, Richard. Comin' out again tomorrow?' But his wife more than made up for his stoic demeanour.

Man, she was a noisy woman, all apron and beefy arms and an impressive head of dark curly hair. She laughed until her belly shook, loved to play games with us kids — action games where you had to chant anatomical parts while pointing to said part as the list got longer and longer. What the hell was that called? Ah, it just came to me: 'Alouette, gentille Alouette/Alouette, je te plumerai. Je te plumerai la tête' and so on. 'Little skylark, lovely little skylark,

I will pluck you. I will pluck the feathers from your head' — and from your nose, your neck, your tummy, etc. What a strange song, famous in Canada.

As you worked your way down the body, plucking the feathers off the poor lark, you had to remember all the locations and chant them out loud while pointing to the appropriate body part with two hands. The list grew longer and exhaustingly longer as you went, and it was keeping up that was the fun, the challenge. We would all sit round the feet of this intriguing woman and bellow these strange French words as loudly as we could, while she laughed and shrieked fit to bust.

The Winchester girls were a lively combination too. The older and bolder one was always up for a game of doctors and nurses in their caravan whenever the grown-ups were off playing euchre. This curious game of medical procedure was harmless enough, in an alarmingly confrontational way, until it was suggested that it was now time for the nurses to inspect the doctors. I could never see the logic in this reversal and would recommend we raid the biscuit tins while the supply was unattended, or go to the camp store and check out the blue ice blocks . . . Time, maybe, to close the hospital and go for a swim, or a cold shower.

It was always time for a swim. The sea itself was a bit dicey — that classic Hawke's Bay undertow — but the lagoon was fabulous. A bit like a brackish lake in a quarry, to be honest, but we loved it. The gravel sloped straight down into the deepest bit on the bend before the lagoon ran on down to the sea and you could stretch out and bake like a stranded starfish before simply sliding back into the cool water. The slope also meant that you could crawl back out again like a salamander making its first exploratory steps onto dry land before collapsing onto the hot stones for another bake-off. We would cook until we were done like burnt toast, black alongside the white tide-line of our togs. Woollen togs, with the anti-embarrassment apron. I didn't get my racy satin elastics till the next summer, when I was old enough to really have cause to miss that apron.

The lagoon was the outflow of a cranky old creek that ran out along one boundary of the camping ground and the extensive junkyard belonging to the mysterious family who owned the whole thing. One day we found an old wooden dinghy pulled up in the tangled willows and poplars that bordered the junkyard and the creek and were able to pole it up inland for a spell, as long as we kept bailing furiously. I loved this exploring upriver stuff, heading into the unknown.

All the salty beach fun faded behind us the minute we slipped underneath the road that went on around to Clifton beach and we were suddenly in the countryside, punting past cows gazing gormlessly from the bank and pushing the occasional bloated sheep carcass aside as we nosed further into terra incognita. Daring stuff for about half a mile, before we ran aground in weeds and mud. Then you got out into the muck and heaved the creaking pile of rot around and punted back, through the magic portal to the owners' insane property.

The place was a labyrinth of twisting trails through piles of industrial and domestic bric-a-brac that had outlived its usefulness and had nowhere else to go. We'd got to know a couple of the kids who'd lived in that wonky wonderland all their lives and knew their way to the heart of it. And at the heart of it was a coach — a full-sized stagecoach, so buried in years of junk build-up that it was almost impossible to discern the outside. But the boys knew how to get inside, and it was amazing. It looked just like the inside of all the cowboy stagecoaches you saw in the Saturday morning movies down at the Embassy: two padded bench seats facing each other, buttoned upholstery on the walls and net luggage racks above.

This secret cave became our Famous Five headquarters. We'd smuggle biscuits and barley sugars through our secret trails to the narrow stagecoach door and get down to some serious plotting and planning, though we actually didn't have the faintest idea what this involved. We just did stuff: 'Oh, here's a boat, let's go boating!' or 'There's going to be a talent quest on Saturday night, let's go to that!' Just sitting in that coach daydreaming was enough.

How did it get there? There must have been a last day — the final run up to Wairoa, or Waipawa, or Napier. Then it would've been parked up and the horses unharnessed and put to pasture as the new Bedford bus rolled up the driveway. Who knows.

There definitely was a talent quest on Saturday night, and we all went. Some enterprising soul turned up with a flatbed truck, a microphone and a long extension lead that snaked through the grass to the ablution block. This same truck came around regularly to show short black and white comedies, Laurel and Hardy and so on, from an American label called Castle Films.

I can remember the logo that came up before every clip: a short length of 35mm film arranged on its side so that both ends of the strip curled back on themselves like the turrets on the corners of a castle. The sprockets along the upper edge gave the impression of castellations while the blocky title announced itself in the space between the turrets. I was entranced by this clever bit of double illusion and was probably the only person in the entire camping ground to put it together. My future was sealed.

I seem to have acquired a sort-of girlfriend at this point: Susan Butcher. We sat side by side on a rug laughing at that Laurel and Hardy adventure where their jalopy disappears into a water-filled pothole and Laurel takes the occasion to reach out and scoop up, and drink, a glass of water . . . while he's underwater. Afterwards we walked down to the rickety one-lane bridge that the locals had built over the lagoon so you could get to the beach without getting your feet wet.

Everyone loves a talent quest, don't they? Especially out under the stars with the seagulls squawking, toilets flushing and buckets banging in the background and the participants frozen in fright way up there on the back of the truck, exposed to the world. I remember the boy who won. Not much older than me, he got up there, all on his own, and sang a song by Nat King Cole.

I was stunned; we all were. I didn't think it was possible for a human being to do that, to sound like the stuff coming out of the radio. He sang the whole thing, without moving a muscle, in a voice so high and pure that it seemed clear he *was* too young to fall in love and 'they' were right. He clutched the microphone to his chest with both hands and stared straight ahead to the sunset clouds over the Ruahines. When he won, he sang it again. What a night. And to get home I only had to walk 75 yards past the ablution block and through the narrow stand of coprosmas that sheltered our site.

I don't remember how long we stayed out there — perhaps the entire school holidays. With Dad going into work each day, except for the 'statutories', able to mow the lawns, empty the letterbox and grab a few homebrews, we could've stayed there indefinitely. An endless summer. I certainly wouldn't have minded. I had my books: my *Just Williams*, my Enid Blyton and my Willard Price. I was OK whatever the weather. Because it did rain occasionally. 'Don't touch the canvas, you'll let the rain in!' Dad on his knees in the dark, digging a drain around the tent, muttering and cursing.

One year it *really* rained. It poured for days until Mum and Dad had had enough and we packed up and went home. That night the quiet creek burst its banks and a wall of water went thundering through the campground, straight through our vacant site, sweeping the caravan off its blocks. I lay in my own bed that night, trying to imagine what it would be like if a wall of water came through the door. What would it be like to be tucked up all cosy and warm one minute, then cold, wet and possibly drowned the next? It was impossible to imagine. I was too cosy and warm. And still kissed by the sun.

A skink in the hand.

7

RICHARD ALMOST GETS A BROTHER

Mum and Dad decided to buy me a brother. No one thought to consult me about it and I still don't really know what prompted the whole damn enterprise.

Of course they didn't actually *buy* Ray, but that's what it felt like to me — like getting a very bad present. I've cooked up a reason of my own for this strange gift that may or may not be true, but knowing Dad's homophobia it kind of rings true. I think he was worried that I was going to grow up to be a 'pansy', being constantly surrounded, as I was, by so many sisters. Hence the need for another male in my life.

To be fair, I was starting to display unsettling signs of being a bit arty, and to clinch it I would occasionally walk around with my hands drooping downwards from my extended wrists. God knows where I picked that up from. Mum would smack my wrists when she saw me doing it. They must have talked about such 'worrying signs'. Dad's time at sea would've been quite educational. 'Beware of the bosun,' he used to say — whatever a bosun was. So, one day, they turned up with Ray, a nondescript boy about my height and colouring.

How much plotting went into this mad sociological experiment? My sister Valerie tells me that he was placed in her class, so I guess they'd found a boy a year or so younger than me in a considered bid to preserve my elder status. Well, they got that bit right, but they should've done a psychological test as well. Ray couldn't have been more unlike me if you'd designed it that way. As far as I was concerned, he could've come from Mars.

I suspect that this fostering was a trial run before actual adoption, and so Ray tried incredibly hard to fit in. He even called my mother Mum right from the get-go. How could that be in the fostering rules? It drove me insane. The harder he tried to fit in, the worse it got. I didn't know I could get so angry.

He seemed to have no instinct at all for the seething volcano of rage that was plotting and planning his downfall in the next bedroom. He even thought he was going to be allowed to read my comics. Get your own comics, Ray. You probably only like *Eagle* anyway. When he did buy his own, he bought the wrong ones, had no idea that the only good *Donald Duck* comics were the Carl Barks ones. How could he not see that? And *The Phantom* and *Mandrake* — he treated them like comics, like kids' stuff. I could tell by the way he read them, skimming and flicking. And he didn't know the difference between the Wilson McCoy illustrations and that bloody Sy Barry's either.

We fought. Over everything. We fought over who would take the compost down to the compost heap. We fought over chopping the kindling. We fought over filling the coal bucket. I don't know what weird circumstances Ray came from but he just didn't seem to understand the fighting rules, the first of which was knowing when to quit, when to cry 'Submit!'

I knew all about submitting, having fought the entire Havelock North bus posse in some mad rite of passage thing I brought upon myself so I could become part of the gang. I fought all five of them one at a time, on consecutive days after lunch on the patch of grass behind the art room. My big move was the bear hug. Move in quick while they were still wondering what I was up to and grab 'em tightly around the waist while grinding my chin into the soft space under the collarbone. Then I bent them over backwards so they had no balance or traction, and dropped them flat when they called 'Submit!'

Worked every time. Except on big Gavin. He wouldn't bend; hugging him felt like hugging a tree. He hardly seemed to notice me fighting him, just threw me on the ground and sat on my head, chatting to me, until the bell rang for class.

But Ray couldn't be conquered. I could be pounding his head with the seat of the swing, yelling out 'Submit! Submit!', and he'd just curl his arms over his head and stay silent, which would only escalate my fury. Without a 'Submit', what do you do? Kill your opponent? It did cross my mind.

A few weeks later, in a mighty climactic act, I had a go at him with the lawn mower (the push one, not the petrol one — I wasn't a monster). I was busy mowing the grass strip by the footpath when Ray appeared and decided he was going to do the bit that was visible from the kitchen window, on the off chance that Mum would see him being helpful. He tried to wrench the handle from me just as I'd turned by the driveway and was working my way back up towards the corner. Well, that wasn't going to happen.

In all the shoving and pushing I somehow managed to hoick the machine up onto the fulcrum of my hip and swung the business end of the mower in a low and heavy arc at an astonished Ray. As he turned to flee, the flat of one of the large metal wheels caught him right in the small of his back, launching him out onto the footpath. It wasn't much of a swing, it must be said: his knees suffered more than his back. It was a miracle that I even managed to get the thing off the ground, but the drama of the display had a profound effect on the adoption plans.

By now my loathing of the poor bastard must have become obvious even to my optimistic mother, but this incident must have tripped the switch. My parents called time on the whole affair and Ray was returned to wherever he came from. My princely status in the sisterhood was restored.

I had won. And I never gave it a second thought — until now. What a ghastly performance.

I do remember his one slightly redeeming feature: his curious obsession with nature. His bedroom was like a zoo. Shoeboxes of skinks and other small animals, holes punched in the lid, lined his wardrobe. Yolk pooled all over his homework table where he'd blow his egg collection, putting them in cotton wool-lined boxes. There were nests all in a line on the top of the wardrobe. There were baby birds at the end of his bed and *in* his bed. Mum could never figure it out: What was all the discolouration on Ray's sheets? What was with the feathers and twigs everywhere? Not to mention the bird shit. I think he was trying to incubate eggs down there. Did it work?

I don't know, but there were definitely baby birds in his bed. Baby birds and all the mess that goes with them. Maybe that's why Ray slept with his socks on. I thought it was bloody creepy. I had a few nests and bird skulls lying about in my room but I couldn't begin to understand Ray's collection. Why so much?

On more benevolent days we'd cycle out to Te Awanga and fossick in the mingimingi for skinks and whatever else would turn up. We'd cycle home, Ray with a dopey, blissful smile on his face and a school bag full of wildlife. I've got to hand it to him, he had an instinct for the work, albeit a slightly wonky one. He'd catalogue his finds before carrying them out to the rubbish bin. Ray's herpetology had a high turnover rate.

Thinking about it all now, I feel a bit wistful. Maybe he taught me how to value, more keenly, the organic minutiae of our environment. I can't drive past those seaside mingimingi bushes without thinking of Ray. I'll turn to Jude and say, 'There're skinks living in there!'

Maybe we did have something in common, but it would never have been enough.

Many years later, when I was married with three kids and living at Torbay beach, I got a call from Ray. He was in Auckland and wondered if he could come for a visit. Maybe he was looking for a fight? Naturally enough, I was curious to see him again. He turned up in a big old Chevrolet and walked in with a shy young hippy wife and a couple of kids. He reminisced about his stint at 507 as if they were the best years of his life. Was he offering me some sort of absolution? I'm buggered if I know, but I do know he had me beat.

A 1960s Top Flite Space Master kite.

8

FLYING A KITE

If Dad had brought enough meaty rabbits home Mum would make two rabbit pies: one for us and one for the 'poor people' over the road, the Moroneys.

I'm not sure how we knew they were poor. They were certainly scruffier and noisier than us, and there were a lot of them — half-naked toddlers with snotty noses running wild in the backyard like chooks. I was fascinated by them. Their lives seemed to be so random. I mean, Mum knew how to party. One glass of Pimm's No. 1 Cup and she'd have her friends sitting in a row on the floor doing the Māori canoe song — Hawke's Bay housewives rowing across Lake Rotomahana — but the Moroneys seemed to live their life at a completely different pitch. Mum bellowing at Dad, Dad bellowing at the kids, horse racing loud on the radio — they certainly didn't seem to be bothered by being 'poor'.

It was quite a neighbourhood, when I think about it. Possibly the same as any apart from the posh one over by the landscaped carp ponds, but we seemed to have one of everything: the 'poor' Moroneys; the kid down the road with the polio callipers on his skinny legs; the lonely old Scottish bachelor over the other road (we lived on a corner) who was the doctor at the freezing works and who would mercurochrome all our wounds; Shorty Schaffer, next to the Moroneys, who played the piano accordion; and the Robertsons down the road, who invented things, constructing petrol-driven go-karts from scratch and mounting two-way radios on their bicycle carriers.

Next to us, on the empty section side, was a rather stiff but genial schoolteacher named Langford and his very tidy family. He made fretsaw models in his garage and would let me sit there as he demonstrated his skills. Once he made a bus while I watched. All the windows and doors had to be drilled and cut — both sides. Fiddle, fiddle and two deep-flanged cotton reels somehow slotted in for the wheels. He gave me a cut-out sheep standing on a bit of green three-ply. I've still got it.

Lovely man. I would have been surprised if he even had Pimm's No. 1 Cup in the house. The Langfords lived in a prim house, all squared off to the prim flowerbeds and the squared-off paths between. I pulled so many lead-head nails out of the long fence between us for my smelting and casting experiments that it ultimately sagged into his primulas. He never complained, must have thought it was natural attrition. He put up with a lot, even the smoke from the endless smelting fires.

And so up past the round, roughcast white dome thing in the

middle of the intersection that more or less defined the edge of our patch. What was that for? Nobody seemed to know. It was probably something electrical, but it did lend the neighbourhood an exotic air. Then around back towards our place, past the overgrown bungalow where an unmarried mother had died in 'mysterious circumstances'. I used to stand on the footpath trying to stare in past the foliage and through the grimy windows of the deserted sunporch into the dark interior, hoping to get a hint of what might have happened inside.

If I turned left again before I got to our place I could head off up past the traffic cop's fascinating flat-roofed white concrete house with the rounded-off window bay and the little geometric designs over the doors. Flashiest house on the block, his shiny police coupe parked almost mathematically out front.

This intimate little cluster of experience was all in the two or three blocks north of us. Funny how that border was so close, while the southern border managed to extend way out to the town's boundary on the other side of the great rambling borderless mess that was Windsor Park. And right on that boundary, south of the endless digging for the much-anticipated skating rink, was the Jacobs sawmill, with its mountains of ancient sawdust packed and weathered to the consistency of Pinex wallboard. We used to tunnel into it, right into it. Make cave huts and burn candles. I'm bloody lucky to be sitting here writing about it.

Then there was the mossy old artesian swimming pool in the park, which was cold all year. The startlingly graphic graphite graffiti on the studs and dwangs of the rough-and-ready roofless changing sheds contributed to a highly charged back-of-the-bike sheds atmosphere. I crept into the girls' shed one day and found the decorations were just as hair raising.

Occasionally, just to complete the Ronald Hugh Morrieson vibe, the local spook, Snoogles, would go pedalling past like a nightmare wind-up tin toy on his big black bike. The legend was that he would 'get you', but I don't think Snoogles could've got anything. He rode his bike just this side of a wobble, long praying mantis legs going only hard enough to keep him vertical, his grey, beaky face thrust out from a long greasy coat, eyes shining dimly from the shadow of his old fedora. Poor old Snoogles. What did he do to deserve his creepy reputation?

Snoogles' random itinerary takes us back to the more immediate neighbourhood and my own beat past the dairy, chemist, butcher and fish shop to the family who lived behind an inward-leaning corrugated iron fence (wasn't me) that you had to wedge your way through like a kid sneaking into a baseball game. I had a school friend in there: Raymond. He was diligent, softly spoken and minded his own business, but to my overactive imagination the whole place reeked of skulduggery. Big gum trees grew right up against the house, giving the impression of holding it up. Missing verandah boards, sash windows jammed open with blocks of four-by-two. Evidence of absence throughout the house: full ashtrays on the arms of mismatched couches and armchairs, open packs of butter on the crumb-covered table, half-full bottles of milk on the cluttered kitchen bench. In our house, all evidence of every meal had to vanish totally when we'd finished.

His dad seemed cheerful enough in a roguish sort of way, shouting out from somewhere in the dim interior, 'G'day, Richard.

Might be best if you stayed out there on the verandah. Mind the step.'

Raymond had an older brother, Tony, who was a character, an instigator. Shorter than Raymond, but wider, he walked like a spinning top, his arms arched out from his body and his fists softly clenched and curled slightly inwards. Looking for trouble. Tony led bold initiatives like games of shanghai warfare — and more on that later — over in the diggings of the skating rink. He had that gypsy charisma that was hard to say no to.

One day, Tony got onto some paper kites that had just come into a toy store in town. Brightly decorated with comic book illustrations of outer space, the moon and Saturn swirling about. I suspect he got his with the old five-digit discount. Raymond also got one, most likely with actual money, and a couple of the other guys turned up with theirs as well. I was the only one without a bloody kite — and I *had* to have one.

So I stole some money from Mum. Sneaked into her bedroom when she was out, got her purse out of the bedside table and helped myself to a shilling. Presumably I thought adults had so much money sloshing around that Mum would never notice one missing coin. Surely. But things must have been tighter in the Frizzell finances than I could ever have counted on. She confronted me that evening when I got home from the park. 'Have you been stealing from my purse, Richard? Wait till your father gets home!'

And wait I did, praying that he'd drive into a lamppost on the way. But home he got — and pissed as usual, which didn't help. It was hard to know what he was most angry about, me stealing the money or the unwanted interruption to his fuzzy domestic routine.

The ultimate punishment in our house was to be bent bare-arsed over the bath and given a furious walloping with a seriously heavy leather dog collar that lived on a hook beside the Columbus radio. The magnitude of my crime was such that I was also banished to the big old garage down the back of the section. I sat there, sideways, on the oily floorboards, sobbing pitifully, big chest-rattling sobs, for God knows how long. Eventually — it felt like days later — Dad came out onto the back verandah and shouted, 'That's enough!'

I don't know what happened to the kite. I have a dim memory of shamefacedly taking it back, with Mum. I do remember, very vividly, that it had flown like a dream, my little kite-shaped bit of cartoon cosmos up there in a loose row with Tony's and Raymond's. Free as a bird and softly fluttering.

The Hastings Municipal Building staircase.

9

SAVE THE LAST DANCE FOR ME

Philip Morris was a stylish bugger. He sauntered into our lives sometime in the fourth form, looking like a mini Tony Curtis: tousled black forelock falling over one eye, with that stupid school cap pushed so far back in order not to spoil the duck-tail cut that you wondered how it stayed on his head. I'd never seen anyone looking like they should be smoking without actually smoking. Perhaps it was his name. In my usual vampiric way I immediately recognised a natural primitive with a sense of original style that I could never quite master on my own.

We became a sort of double act, walking round town dressed in cobbled-together approximations of whatever latest style Phil had picked up on. Our biggest and most successful statement was Ivy League, a bizarre sort of rock'n'roll version of American bebop campus cool: a vertical black and white striped shirt, tight white pants with an odd buckle arrangement in the middle of the back and a lightweight black and white striped linen cheesecutter cap, also with a buckle doing absolutely nothing at the rear. God knows where we got all this stuff from, or even if we had it right, but it certainly looked different.

I even managed to get my blond crewcut to grow out into a reasonable facsimile of Phil's lustrous pile. The top was trimmed flat like a buxus hedge with the sides left to grow long enough to be swept up and back into a duck's arse and the front allowed to curve forward over the forehead. It required lots of maintenance, and the bloody school cap didn't help, leaving an annoying groove across the perfect plane of the flat-top.

Phil was with us because his dad had taken over the management of the Grand Hotel, a big two-storeyed pile in the middle of the town's main street. And this, of course, was the most exotic thing about my new friend: he lived in a hotel. Not behind it or next to it, but *in* it. Until then I'd never even been through the door of a hotel. I'd stood outside waiting on the footpath while someone went inside to fetch Dad but this was something entirely new.

We ate upstairs at the top table in the dining room, which was like a large restaurant — another mysterious establishment I'd never experienced. We did the whole thing: table settings and menus. You could choose what you wanted to eat and waiters brought it to you. Or waitress in this case, a young, shy Māori girl called Bunny, who seemed to be there to wait exclusively on the top table. It gives me a strange thrill to write her name down after all these years. I thought I was in love with her. She was obviously two or three years older than me and never gave me the slightest sign that she even knew I was there, apart from avoiding all eye contact and becoming oddly panicked whenever she served me.

That was a sign, wasn't it? I followed her round like a sick puppy, always with some lame excuse to be in or near the kitchen. Philip figured it out and might even have said something to her because I definitely sensed a shift in her attention. This may, of course, have been delusional — occasionally easing her way closely past me in the kitchen was hardly a rampant display of affection. Nevertheless I started plotting how to come face to face with her. I knew she lived in a row of staff bedrooms near the laundry but manoeuvring myself out there seemed a trick beyond imagining.

Then, right on cue came my big break: the end-of-year school ball — two or three hours of mingled confusion. I'd sneak out of the dance, hoof it down the few blocks to the pub, climb the fire escape and knock on Bunny's door. Then, after God knows what, I'd sneak back to the ball.

The night of the ball I busied myself in the hall, bustling about checking my *Alley Oop* decorations: a squat cartoon caveman in a leopard-skin off-the-shoulder singlet, clutching a huge club and peering out from beneath a shaggy fringe. Then at some chaotic moment between the foxtrot and the quickstep, I slipped off down the stairs, the Spanish Mission stairs, and headed north up the back streets (change of plan) to the rear of the Grand Hotel. I scuffed around in the gravel for a spell, trying to slow my breathing down. Then, in what fit of madness I can't now imagine, the mad prowler, in his school uniform and blazer, climbed up the fire escape and knocked on Bunny's door.

Bunny, in her nightie, opened the door, then went back and sat on the bed. I somehow got across the threshold, closed the door and sat down next to her. And that was pretty much it. I couldn't move and Bunny showed no sign of moving. How long did we sit there in the dim light of her bedside lamp? Do I have a memory of touching her nightied back, the feeling of warm skin through winceyette? Did I really do that? After a minute or two of mute and mutual panic I got to my feet and silently mooched off into the night.

I climbed back up the Spanish steps, went into the hall past my cardboard caveman lurking in his cardboard jungle, and merged into the throng just in time for the ridiculous Maxina. The great lothario returned. All the girls looked like children after my exotic waitress. I'd pretty much gone back to my normal, nerdy state by the time the hall was cleared for the Gay Gordons.

This curious and ancient Scottish folk dance was a chance for everybody to get up and have a go. It required the formation of two huge circles, with the boys going one way and the girls going the other. It was a sort of chain reaction thing where the opposing two met and twirled each other in a brief dosey-doe that somehow passed both partners on to two more. You'd meet the love of your life, hold her lightly, fantasise for a second, before sending her on to the next oaf and reaching out for a girl you'd usually run a mile to avoid.

I was just giving a plump little girl called Peanut a twirl when the guy behind me (Melvin Fuller, if you're interested) gave me a tap on the shoulder and said, 'Hey, Richard, it's your mother.' I dropped Peanut's little hand with its wadded-up handkerchief and turned in the direction of Melvin's eye-popping stare. And here's the thing: at this particular point in the stupid dance, I happened to be bang up against the stage end of the hall, far away from the big double entry doors. Which meant, of course, that anyone wanting to traverse the ring of merry dancers had to walk the entire length of the hall, through the vacant area in the middle.

And that's just what my mother was doing. She'd obviously decided that I'd been out roistering quite long enough and she'd come to get me. There she was, in curlers and gauzy head scarf, slippers and plum-coloured dressing gown fringed with nightie, sailing across the empty acres of dance floor directly towards me. The music stopped, the Scottish chain reaction ground to a halt and everyone watched as Mum led me (I'd like to say by the ear but I don't think it came to that) back across the hall, down the Spanish steps and out into the street to the waiting Austin.

The strangest thing about this humiliation was that I never got razzed for it. Such was the level of my indignity, I won the sympathy vote. But my mates did remind me of it throughout the summer holidays.

And Bunny, what happened about my unrequited love affair with Bunny? She continued to serve me stewed fruit and ice cream as if nothing had ever happened — and I suppose nothing really had. Philip, though, seemed convinced that something had transpired, and threw us both curiously baited looks. He'd missed the spectacle at the dance, being far too sophisticated for anything as square as a school ball.

His fashion sense went on to evolve into something more leathery and bodgie-like while I morphed from Ivy League into a try-hard beatnik look, which pretty much signalled the fading of the friendship. It was doomed anyway. There was no way Philip was going to follow me to university. And neither was Bunny.

On the way up.

10

THE PEAK

Everyone in Hawke's Bay knew 'The Peak' — Te Mata Peak. Especially those of us in Hastings who could see it on the skyline behind Havelock North any time we cared to glance in that direction.

Well, I *think* we were looking at the Peak. What we were actually looking at was a fascinating range of hills in the shape of a giant man lying on his back, with his head pointing west towards Waipawa and his feet pointing east out into the bay.

There was some degree of ambiguity as to which part of the sleeping giant's anatomy actually formed the Peak, the highest point on the range because the trig station was up there, but quite where it lay in the giant's obvious profile was hard to determine from down on the plain. The bit that looked most like a peak was right where the giant's penis would be, but no one would actually say it. My mother was convinced that it formed the giant's knee. Maybe it was just me. We see what we want to see.

Of course there's a Māori story — well, more than one — behind the name, though the well-known legend says that it's the prostrate body of the rangatira Te Mata of Waimārama lying across the landscape, after having to prove his love to his hostage bride Hinerākau by biting a quick route to Waimārama through the hills from the Heretaunga Plains and then choking on a mouthful of limestone.

Every visitor from out of town — irritating relatives who needed to be distracted for an hour or two, or friends from the big smoke who were obviously short of outstanding geological experiences — had to go 'up the Peak'. And it was, indeed, impressive, no matter how often, or for what reason, we made the trip. You seemed to be able to see half the North Island. You could definitely see Mount Ruapehu, which was about two days' drive away.

Back in the mid-1950s it was a hell of a thing to get up, via a narrow gravel road with not a lot of leeway on either side. I'm not sure what happened when a car going up met a car coming down, but I seem to remember a lot of backing up.

My mates and I pedalled up, though we can't have done much actual pedalling, even on the way down — more braking than pedalling, if you had brakes. I know I didn't. My sad old junkyard Frankenstein was what they called a fixed-wheeler, whose large chain sprocket at the pedal end had no gearing whatsoever connecting it to the smaller sprocket at the wheel hub end.

Whatever the hub did, the pedal sprocket followed. And it never stopped.

If the bike went into freewheel on a steep slope (or any slope, come to that) and your feet lost contact with the pedals, you never got them back on again. All you could do was hang on — with your feet well wide of the frantically whirling pedals — and if you needed to stop for any reason you had to jam your feet down into the gravel, or hurl yourself sideways into the grassy bank. Mostly it didn't matter because Hastings is as flat as a pancake, but it was dynamite up on the Peak's switchbacks.

Getting right to the top of the Peak was usually the least of it anyway. Mostly we were there for the caves. You couldn't see them from the road, even if you were standing there and someone tried to point them out. We would lie our bikes down in the long grass just off the road, climb down the slope to an old stand of pōhutukawa at the base of the decline and crawl through the shadow of the trees to a narrow, fern-shrouded cleft that burrowed directly back into the bank through the tangled tree roots. I'm told that the old limestone formations up there are riddled with caves, and that may be so, but this one was the real deal. This was 'our' cave.

The first 50 yards or so were OK, but then it started to get a bit scary. It narrowed, from top to bottom, until you had to get down on your hands and knees for a spell before it really closed in and you were obliged to imitate a lizard and propel yourself forward with your elbows. I can't remember if I was too panicked to be excited, or too excited to panic. I do know that pretending you were tunnelling out of a German POW camp took away some of the anxiety, as did the progress of the heels in front of you . . . and the obvious signs of general wear on the roof and walls of the wormhole exposed by the light of the torch.

The other thing that terrified me in the confined space was my sheath knife. These were a bit of a thing at the time — a hangover from the Davy Crockett fad that swept the country. The coonskin hat had faded away, but the knife lingered on. And I had one: in its sheath, on my belt. I'd read, or heard, somewhere, about a boy crawling through a culvert that somehow narrowed to a point where he couldn't go forward, and, as he tried to back up, his sheath knife caught in a join in the pipes and he couldn't go back either. So I took the knife off my belt before we went in and put it in my school bag with my lunch, and pushed it along before me, hot on Simon's reassuring heels.

It seemed to go on way too long, though. I couldn't stop thinking of the entire weight of the Peak just inches above my back. And then it suddenly opened up. The space must have been two or three storeys high, and about as deep again as the distance we'd just traversed.

Of course if I could go back now for a look it'd probably be about the size of the big shed back at 507, but I do know it was dramatic — the torchlight suddenly shooting up and out into the craggy, rock-lined space. I also knew that we weren't the first to get there. The walls were covered with ancient cave art: 'SM loves CP town bike.' What the hell did that mean? Basically it looked like the boys' changing shed at the Windsor Park swimming pool, with lots of that peculiar glyph that I was only just starting to figure out: a capital W overlaid with a capital M and crudely embellished with dangling adornments.

There were a couple of interesting fissures at the farthest end of the space, but we were quite happy to call it quits and treat our big discovery as our final destination. How much life was left in those torch batteries? We ate our lunch, added to the wall art and wriggled our way out again. Going out, of course, was easier than going in. Almost an anti-climax really. Bright sunlight, blue sky and yellow grass, Hawke's Bay heat.

Further down the small ravine a spring bubbled up through the limestone, and if we followed it on downhill, which we invariably did, to where it swelled into a more substantial creek, we could catch freshwater crayfish, kōura. I don't think we ever quite knew what to make of them. It certainly never occurred to us that you could eat them. Eat something from a creek? It'd be as mad as trying to eat a cockabully or an eel.

But they were a hell of a thing to find: a dark sort of mottled green bug hiding among the stones under the bank and hard to see, which probably made the discovery feel more significant. And they were so unexpected, these miniature lobsters. Because that's what they looked like, American lobsters, complete with the classic claws, but about the size of a large prawn. Totally alien beings up there in the hills. Once we'd waved them about a bit and tried to get them to pinch someone there was nothing much else you could do with them.

Years later I travelled through the deep south of America and ate mountains of them: crawfish, fiddly as prawns. Elvis even sang about them. It was a good thing we didn't regard them as edible back then because one good feed among five boys would've cleaned the creek out.

The other merry old pastime, once we'd got sick of wading in the creek, was dry-grass tobogganing. Mostly just a sheet of corrugated iron with a turn-up at one end, they certainly didn't *look* like toboggans and I doubt that we even called them by such a fancy American name, though we certainly knew it, thanks to our comics. I think we just called them sleds, if we called them anything at all. Sheets of corrugated cardboard did pretty much the same job but were a pain to take up there all the time because they just rotted away in the grass.

Those sheets of iron were a horrifying prospect. I'm surprised none of us were decapitated. We were certainly dinged about a lot as rider and sled parted company and the riderless guillotine continued on, careering down the hill.

All of this — the mad freewheeling, the cave, the kōura and the sledging — were hardly daily events, as it was quite a hike from my place in Hastings over there by Windsor Park. But the Huckleberry Finn sense of adventure was real. The packed lunch, the ride out to Havelock, meeting the boys in the village and the long grind up from the private boys' school at the bottom of the road to the Peak.

The smell of all that hot, dry grass. The white, dusty limestone grinding down the soles of your feet as you attempted to brake after turning back because you overran the cave spot. The blessed coolness of the creek. The fabulous exhaustion at the end of it all and the comfortable thrill of still being alive as you rode home at dusk along the 6-mile stretch of orchards and fruit stalls that connected Havelock North to Hastings, with that damn fixed wheel obliging the knees to never stop pumping.

Difficult details.

11

BREAKING THE MOULD

My mother said 'bugger' once. Not just once; she said it three times: 'Bugger, bugger, bugger'.

We'd just had an earthquake — one of those good old Hawke's Bay rattlers — and it had shaken all her preserved peaches off the pantry shelves. I found her standing in a sea of broken glass, peach quarters and red preserving rings, stamping one foot and with clenched fists raised. This was a big moment. I'd never heard her swear before. She hated it. The boys on the back verandah had to really behave themselves when they gathered for the Saturday morning brew.

I was going to say, by way of furthering this narrative, that Mum had to put up with a lot, but apart from Dad's boozing I think we had it pretty good. It definitely wasn't a glum household. Dad would've been making a decent quid and he had a bloody good mortgage, thanks to his sisters. In fact, years later, he told me that if he'd realised what a great wicket he was on he would've dragged it out a bit and we could've had more fun.

Mum loved a good joke, even if it was on her. She always had a hell of a job getting me out of bed in the weekends. The threats from the kitchen would get more and more strident: 'Don't lie there stinking all day'; 'If you don't get up in a minute I'm coming in with the strap!'

One morning I got out of bed, did the prison escape trick of making a human shape under the covers with my pillows, and hid behind the door. Not long after the final ultimatum she came into my room and started whaling away at the eiderdown with the dog collar. I stepped out from behind the door and said, 'What are you doing, Mum?' When she got over her heart attack she thought it was quite funny and was probably planning how to restage it at her kindergarten mothers' club drama group.

Apart from amateur theatrics, Mum's big thing was craft, and always had been. She'd gone straight to art school from high school in a curiously smooth transition that somehow didn't really seem like a great academic decision. In fact, she told me that half her hockey team decided to go along with her. Seems like everyone fancied their hand at a bit of craft in those days as they drew little Victorian silhouettes of bluebells and fairies in one another's autograph books and designed monograms to embroider on their blazers.

I suspect Mum quickly pulled ahead of the jolly hockey sticks crowd with her focus on the business of design and finish. I've still got some of her notebooks and examination samples and I marvel at the level of professionalism she reached. She never seemed to be bothered with anything like an artistic thought or, if she was, never let on about it. She just loved applied art, though I doubt she would've called it that.

Mum applied art to everything. She would trace a Goldie portrait, grid it up, transcribe it onto a shallow wooden bowl and render it in gouache with astonishing fidelity. I used to sit and watch her do it, dipping the brush into the water, refining the point with a little lick from pursed lips before dotting the white highlights onto the kuia's chin whiskers. She did the same with Buller's birds and with botany — sprays of kōwhai and raupō reeds in the swamp, all without the slightest interest in who the original artists were. Totally without guile. Everything was just stuff in the world, put there for Mum's delectation.

Watching her do these magic rendering tricks was strange because she would drift off into a space far, far away from the aproned woman with a blue rinse responsible for a functioning alcoholic and, eventually, six kids.

When Dad met her she was working in a handbag workshop in Auckland's Grafton Gully, designing, cutting and embellishing a snappy range of bags in all manner of shapes and persuasions. Felt fold-overs decorated with appliquéd felt rose petals and generously welted seams all stitched in line on the bias. Or, if in leather, fantails pokerworked lightly onto the outside flap.

Dad used to tell us a lovely story about the moment he knew he wanted to marry Mum. They were walking in the Auckland Domain, Mum all decked out in a stylish new hat. When it started to rain, Dad went into a spin and suggested they get a bit of a wriggle on and scamper up to the Wintergardens for shelter. It seems that scampering wasn't going to happen in front of the dashing new engineer boyfriend so Mum said, 'Don't worry, it's only a hat.'

Isn't that great?

How long Mum kept her skills going in the early days of the marriage I have no idea, but I do know that by the time I was six or seven she was in full production. Lots of those Goldie bowls, the tracings looking pretty distressed by now. Lots of kingfishers on swampy boughs, all French-polished and distributed among friends.

Then there was a side business in all manner of strange and exotic items, like felt Egyptian friezes, plaster fish in pastel dots blowing plaster bubbles up the bathroom wall, plaster Bambis in the living room. The inspiration for this avalanche of kitsch probably came out of the *New Zealand Woman's Weekly* — pull-out patterns of pig-shaped breadboards and Pinocchio puppets, all to scale. The breadboards had a big run. Mum commissioned the carpenters at the freezing works to cut out the blanks and she would etch in the tertiary details with an old pokerwork machine she'd salvaged from somewhere. We loved this lethal-looking instrument and would cover anything wooden in the toy box with burnt brown doodles fringed with umber edging. Sst, sst, sst. The machine's looped stylus glowing red hot and the kitchen reeking of scorched wood.

The other kitchen-table fun was moulds. Mum loved those. It must have been one of those fads, like hula hoops, that swept through the country periodically. But the Frizzells took this one very seriously. The whole shemozzle: the plaster of paris, the mixing, the pouring, the squeezing for bubbles, we did it all. The mess was fantastic. The distinctive red rubber moulds themselves were mostly of Disney characters with the odd ring-ins like Popeye and a crusty old seadog complete with pipe, beard, hands deep in pea-jacket pockets and feet firmly planted on his plaster mound. The pipe didn't stick out as pipes do because it would've been beyond the technical reach of the rubber mould and so the pipe had to sort of lie flat on the beard. Quite a tricky detail to paint.

To create the figure the mould had to be inverted into an appropriately sized jar, braced with a cardboard collar at the pouring end to stop the weight of the plaster dragging the whole thing in. Then the wet, white gloop was poured in, right to the brim, and left overnight after a bit of the squeezing for bubbles. The next day you took it out of the jar, discarded the collar and gently peeled back the rubber and there it would be, all in ghostly white, your Scrooge McDuck or Dopey — hopefully with no air bubbles.

Then, of course, came the best bit: the painting. I loved this as much as Mum; in fact we all did. She would sit at the table with us, correcting our mistakes and splatters, tipping in the difficult details like Snow White's eyelashes. She would hold the figure up off the table with one hand and apply the finishing touches with the other: brush held delicately on the horizontal, head tossed back as she aimed down the ferrule with eyes squinted while we laboured away at table-top level. I had my specialities: that sea captain, and Pluto, Goofy and Uncle Scrooge. Mum and my sisters could have Snow White and the dwarfs.

Mum even went so far as to have them varnished, even the dodgy ones, though on reflection they all looked pretty good. Because Mum made sure of it. None of this modern 'salute the child's creative effort' stuff. Mum was all about finish. She got a carpenter from the freezing works to build a special display unit into the redundant door that used to connect the kitchen–dining room with the peaches pantry. The finished line-ups looked like a wonky Wedgwood display, colourful and shiny, all the characters in their appropriate family groups.

One weekend Mum and Dad went off somewhere for a wedding and I was left in charge. Where were my sisters? I have no idea, but it looked like I was getting Saturday night to myself and so I asked the usual gang of hooligans over for the evening. They duly turned up and we went through the usual ritual of sitting around shooting the shit with a flagon of beer clamped between our ankles.

So far, so good, until Simon lurched to his feet and suggested a game of darts. Dad had set the board up on a sheet of Pinex right between the door into the kitchen and the repurposed door into the pantry. Yes, *that* door, the one that had became a display case for a priceless collection of painted plaster moulds.

The game, five individuals, three darts each, started out in a relatively sane and sensible manner until one of us hooked a shot and the dart went right into Popeye's bright white belt buckle. Now, for some godforsaken *Lord of the Flies* reason this startling moment of real targeting swung the drunken hoons' attention, mine included, to the display. To the moulds.

We went nuts, hurling all our darts at the three-dimensional cartoon parade in a furious fusillade. You didn't aim, didn't think, just threw everything you had at the moulds. It was like those games at the Easter Show — all those happy characters just asking for it. We didn't retrieve our darts and have another go. As soon as they had all left our hands the frenzy abated. It didn't last long, probably only a minute, but the results were dramatic. A plaster of paris Pearl Harbor. Bits of dwarf everywhere, pointy divots out of Snow White's gown. Goofy's hat down on the floor next to Pluto's head gazing happily up from a scattering of plaster chips.

The boys suddenly remembered they had things to avoid doing the next day and gathered up their empty flagons (2 shillings return) and buggered off. After standing there feeling like the worst criminal in the history of criminals, I eventually gathered up the bits, sorted them into the relevant piles and swept up the chips. It didn't look too bad when I'd finished. We'd missed a lot, which meant lots of holes in the dark varnished wood, which I was able to burnish over. But there was no denying the somewhat diminished nature of the display. I crept off to bed and lay there in dread.

And, yep, I got it. Again. It wasn't as bad as the money stealing incident; Dad obviously didn't give a shit about the moulds. He probably would have paid me to throw them all out so he wouldn't have to stare at them when he came home for lunch.

Mum was remarkably staunch about it too. Maybe she saw it as a challenge, because my follow-up punishment was to restore them all. And Mum joined in. It was quite a lovely project. Gluing them all back together. Sprucing up Snow White's gown. Bogging up the divots. Getting Pluto's head back on. I think Mum and I bonded over the plaster, the paint and the varnish, quietly working away on our restoration project at the kitchen table, seeing out the plaster mould fad, putting all those floppy red rubber sleeves away to perish at the back of the broom closet.

Dad moved the dartboard out to the garage.

The author's friend preparing the vittles.

12

BAN IRIGHAM

I've changed his name to protect the innocent. Not that Ian needs any protection and I doubt he was ever innocent of anything.

It was his idea to switch the first letters of our names. I became Frick Dizzell for about five minutes, but Ban Irigham seemed to last longer. Perhaps it was the inferences in the word 'ban'; shit did not stick to that boy. He wasn't egregious, smarmy or slick. Not a conman or a seducer. Well, he might have been a seducer; he was certainly a hell of a charmer. He could look at adults in a weird smiley-faced way, shake their hands, look them in the eye with his face thrust forward and have them eating out of the palm of the hand he'd just led with.

He turned up at Hastings Boys' High School halfway through the third form. Our first year. The headmaster delivered him to our class and the form teacher directed him to the empty desk right next to me where I got the instant, 'How do you do? My name is Ian' treatment. Boom. Just like that he was part of the gang. Our leaderless rabble suddenly had a leader.

I'm not sure how he rose to the top of the ranking like that. He just did it. Bought a guitar and taught himself to play it so he could lead the singing at our riverside bonfire booze-ups, which also put him front and centre around the fire. He must have had savings or something because at some point he decided he needed a room of his own — for the guitar and the girls (yes, he *was* a seducer) — and so he built one out the back of the garage. How the hell do you do that while you're still going to high school?

But build a room he did: foundations, joists, studs, dwangs, rafters, tin and a door and a window. He got hold of a book on carpentry from somewhere and got straight into it. I've no idea where he got the materials from but the damn thing just rose up out of the ground almost as we watched. He even built bunks into it. One minute there were just a couple of struggling mint bushes and a rusting incinerator in the vacant space, and the next we were all lying on the bunks reading *Men Only* magazines and listening to Ian teach himself how to play 'Tom Dooley' on his big yellow guitar.

School just seemed like something he did for the hell of it, humouring the teachers with his fake sincerity thing, gazing up with a deep-listening frown on his face, head slightly tilted, as he said, 'Is that right, sir? How interesting!' If I'd pulled a stunt like that I would've been walloped.

He was one of those walking-with-elbows-out kind of guys. He'd strike oddly courtly poses, perfectly natural to him, whenever he delivered one of his worldly observations: one elbow raised behind him, forearm down with palm out and down, while leading with the front shoulder slightly dropped, the other palm up and extended towards you. His long trowel-shaped face would be perfectly vertical, his wide mouth delivering with serious purpose.

And his pronouncements always carried the weight of authority, even when he was lying down on his bunk: 'Girls like having their nipples massaged.' Where did he get *that* from? I certainly didn't know enough to take issue with any of it. Where had he been before turning up in Hastings? Borstal?

I don't think Mum and Dad trusted Ian entirely. Just too charming altogether. Maybe they thought he was going to lead me astray. Ha, as if I was ever going to keep up with Ian Brigham.

He once generously offered to give Dad a hand bringing in the latest crop of potatoes from the big piece of vacant land that made up half of our section. Dad would advance along the row with his potato fork, turning over the plants while we followed along behind, sifting the potatoes out of the loosened soil. That year the entire crop had been hit by a pretty serious blight and the yield was minimal, to say the least, but smart-arse Brigham would periodically call out, 'Great crop you've got here, Mr Frizzell, almost as many as you put in!' At one point I thought Dad was going to ding him with the shovel but Ian's timing was always perfect. He knew when to stop.

We formed a small skiffle band, me on Mum's tea-chest bass, Ian on guitar and an interesting friend called Johnny Dick on bongos. Johnny only had a thumb and little finger on his left hand but it never seemed to slow him down. In fact, years later, he went on to play drums with Max Merritt and the Meteors, who started out in New Zealand and then crossed the Tasman. We never played in public, hardly ever played at all to be honest, just horsed around in Ian's shed — more 'Tom Dooley' — and dreamt about it. We called ourselves The Brothers Mad, *Mad* magazine being the big style arbiter of the time, and I've got a drawing somewhere of the three of us earnestly thumping away, all wearing matching T-shirts with the *Mad* M on the front. I signed the drawing 'Dik Frizzell', also in the hipster spirit of the time.

The two of us got jobs as the milkman's slaves, Ian on one side of the road and me on the other, jogging back and forth from the letterboxes and the slow driving truck, switching out the empty milk bottles for the full ones, milky water in our palms as we shook the tokens out of the half-rinsed bottles.

Our run went from the original edge of town, over behind the big park and the sawmill and out into a smart new suburb where the asparagus fields used to be. The old wooden houses suddenly gave way to faux Californian split-level bungalows in Summerhill stone (long, lie-flat white bricks with the occasional swish diagonal mortar joint) and very shallow pitched roofs. I was quite intrigued by this architectural upgrade, but Ian seemed utterly entranced. He called them homes, while I insisted that they were houses.

A house only becomes a home when you're living in it. We almost came to blows over it. What sort of gulf between us did it actually represent? And he *was* sentimental, seriously sentimental, though I also knew what a ruthless ratbag he could be. An odd friendship, but then I guess all my friendships were rather 'other-ish'. Me just pretending to be a normal, regular human.

Round about the fifth form, school was proving to be too restrictive for Ian. He'd already put a deposit on a small section out at the edge of town and was growing his own blight-free potatoes on it. Said he'd build a house there when he got married and I had no reason to doubt him. High school wasn't going to carry Ian any further and he left without waiting for any exam results or the end of term. He got a job as an auto-electrical apprentice with Hector Jones, over on the far side of town, got himself some grey overalls and became an adult.

We still saw each other in the weekend, when I put my long pants on, but the social disparity became increasingly obvious. I'd call into the garage on the way home from school to organise a movie or whatever and Ian would emerge from under the hoist or the pit, clutching a shifting spanner and covered in grease, while I stood there in my uniform feeling about 10 years old. He started to get serious girlfriends about this time, too, while I was still struggling with the manoeuvres required to hold a girl's hand. When I went off to art school in Christchurch that was pretty much the end of that.

Ian married a nice Havelock girl, moved to Sydney and somehow magically morphed from an auto electrician into the manager of a very trendy seventies hotel on William Street called the Boulevard, which had windows stacked like rows of *Jetsons* TV sets. We stayed there once as his guests. Very flash: John Rowles seated across from us at dinner, cocktails on the roof. And bikinis and gold medallions abounding. And extremely busy. When I remarked on the size of the crowd to Ian, who was posing grandly in his tan suit, he said his pool was the only one in town with water in it. New South Wales was in the grip of a serious drought and water for pools was a serious luxury, but my creative friend had drained the emergency fire tank into the pool, and prayed for no fires. His prayers worked — they had always seemed to — and Ian glided through the summer as the manager of the most profitable hotel on the strip. He'd done it again.

The author with three of his sisters:
Valerie to his left, Tonie front
left and Steve front right.

13

FIRST OF SIX

I don't think I was too much of a prick. All of us kids seemed to muddle along OK. But then I wouldn't know, being the oldest, the first born, the only boy — for as long as this story lasts anyway.

Dad had come ashore when I was born. Then he waited for the second boy. Nope, it was a girl. OK, fair enough, he could handle that, and they called her Valerie. So they had another go. Oops, another girl, but as a gesture of hope they called her Antonie. Tonie for short. Almost a boy. Alright, next time surely. No deal, another girl. She was christened Stephanie. Steve for short. Getting close.

Then they paused. Could've been a miscarriage, but you'd never know. No one mentioned things like that in those days. No pity sought.

Anyway, after a spell, along came another girl: Lesley. Was Dad serious? I now had one sister and three brothers: Tonie, Steve and Les. It didn't bother me; far from it. Can you imagine how spoilt I was? Not my fault I had to have a separate room while they all got funnelled off, in varying combinations of two, into the big bedrooms up the hall. There was certainly plenty of room: Dad's cheap loan had bought him a villa with lots of square footage. Two verandahs, a porch and a medieval-looking turret on one corner. Heavy stained glass panels around the front door, which hardly ever got used because it was a bit hard to distinguish from all the other 'front' doors.

Because the house stood on a corner, the approach was something of a mystery. The letterbox was situated right on the corner where the two streets intersected, and the path from it ran between two even triangles of landscaping right up to the turret — which had eight windows, two doors, a spire and a finial — at which point it split and took off with equal emphasis down past the northern 'front' verandah and the eastern 'side' verandah. Slightly confusing for the Rawleigh's man.

As a consequence, most of the traffic was directed to the back porch, where all the action happened. This was accessed by a very clearly indicated driveway entrance on the other street that made up the intersection. This was obviously the main gate, but it wasn't our address. The letterbox address that served *both* streets was 507 Sylvan Road, but the 'drive in here' address, with the large milk box, was Victoria Street. Didn't even have a number.

Visitor or resident, you turned in there, drove past the lemon tree and, usually, pulled up at the foot of a narrow concrete path that divided a large rectangle of scrappy grass and ran up to the back porch steps. This was the major junction. This was where the Austin sat for most of the day. But if you cared to, or had forgotten something at the dairy, you could keep on going. Right up towards the mighty garage poised royally at the top of its large concrete ramp, at the foot of which the driveway did a railway switcheroo, and continued around the far corner of what we called 'the section', past the path up to the woodshed, underneath the monster walnut tree, down between the fence-of-very-few-nails and the asparagus beds, skirting the leading edge of a boxthorn hedge, over the pavement and the culvert . . . and back out onto the street.

Except for the turret, the house was more or less symmetrical, the left-hand layout echoing the right. A grand hallway marched down the middle from the massive front door, whose lock was as big as a bound volume of *Beano*, until it made a T intersection with a lesser hall that fed the business end of the house, with the kitchen/dining room at one end, the boarder's room at the other and my cubby hole and the bathroom in between.

The back porch followed the same arrangement, with my window and the bathroom window ahead if you were standing on that concrete path looking north up into the porch, the kitchen through the screen door to the right and the washhouse to the left.

The only anomaly was the toilet: a little room of its own that came out onto the porch from the washhouse wall. This sophisticated add-on created a small nook surrounded by the toilet door to the left, the washhouse door straight ahead and my big sash window to the right. Yes, that's right, as I sat at my desk doing my homework or drawing pictures of the Katzenjammer kids, I looked directly into the toilet. Such was my kingdom. Mum would always call out, 'Don't look!' whenever she went, because she seemed to have an issue with shutting the door all the way.

I sat at that desk for 10 or so years, drawing anything that caught my eye. Illustrations from Dad's ancient *Boy's Own Paper*, *Batman* comics . . . I remember when I first said 'Batman' out loud after years of silent reading in my toilet-shaded room and I got such a delicious kick out of it that I would cycle along calling them *all* out loud: 'Batman! Aquaman! Green Arrow! Superman! Flash!'

I would pin the best of these pen and ink renderings to the wall and by the time I left for art school the room was papered with drawings from floor to ceiling. While I was away, Mum threw them all out and repapered the room. Not as any kind of statement, just a spruce-up.

My little room: single bed, desk and dresser, rod and curtain for a wardrobe. Must have been a maid's room back in the day, when massive velvet drapes hung at the entrance to the big hall. I saw them when Mum and Dad went to inspect the place before buying it. I also remember a large taxidermied fox striding out, tail streaming behind him, in a long glass box between the bathroom door and 'my' door. I thought the place was some kind of haunted mansion. The ghosts, and the fox, disappeared the minute we bought it.

So that end of the house was mine. The other end, the front end where the sun was, belonged to my sisters and Mum with all her boxes of dress-ups and swags of sewing. Lots of dresses on hangers and more stuffed in boxes. Dad's ownership of the space was minimal — just his guns clipped to the wall above the bedroom fireplace.

But I had my headquarters. At night I could hear Mum and Dad discussing the day in the bath, splashing and mumbling. Other nights I would sneak the few feet down to the dining room doorway and lie on the floorboards in my dressing gown and listen to the radio playing Tennessee Ernie Ford's 'Sixteen Tons'. It was the first song I heard that made me realise music could *be* something.

I also found that if you were out on the porch, ostensibly going to the toilet past the pearly semolina-textured opaque glass of the bathroom window, and if you squinted hard enough and the light was right, you could almost imagine that you could see the boarder getting in or out of the bath. This was a subterfuge that took impeccable timing, and I was perfectly situated to achieve it.

It also was a great porch for eating apples from the box under the bathroom window and practising the hula-hoop on a rainy day. You know, healthy stuff as well.

But it's Mum's parties that I want to talk about. She loved throwing these big hooleys. Without the need for much of an excuse the house would be full of all manner of mad carousers. Dad would set himself up next to the beer keg on the bench in the kitchen while Mum led the party activities in the big living room. She would brace herself by the kitchen table, pick up the small glass of Pimm's as if she was going to take some evil elixir, purse her lips and knock it back in a couple of gulps.

There'd be a flash of lightning and, shazam, my mother would go from Domestic Mum to Party Mum. With a shudder and a shake of her shoulders she'd march off and plonk herself down in front of our upright piano. Mum pounded on that long-suffering instrument as if she were playing jungle drums, chording out the melody with her right hand while the left randomly thumped away, keeping the beat. The singing was so raucous that no one noticed, or cared.

I was ideally placed, in my hideaway across from the grand junction, to keep an eye on all of it. As long as I didn't open my door too widely I seemed to be invisible. A group of freezing works engineers would burst out of the living room door and tumble off up the hall, laughing and yodelling, to reappear in a minute or two dressed as ballerinas. Mum made them do it. I never saw an actual performance but I could hear them hooting and hollering as they all died like swans.

Joe Woodham would turn up with his guitar and take over music duties as Mum and the whole kindergarten mothers' club headed for the kitchen to get the food ready. Dad reckoned that Joe could strum like a mad bastard, throw the guitar in the air, spin round on the piano seat, whack out a chord or two then spin back and catch the guitar coming down and carry on. And who was I to question such artistry?

The lurching would get more dramatic as the party wore on. Every now and again Dad would appear in my line of sight making his way from the keg to the living room, ricocheting from one side of the hall to the other as he tried to make the last lurch line up with the doorway. Then, if I swivelled my head around, I could watch old Shorty Schaffer from over the road sitting on the back porch steps, serenading the toilet queue with his piano accordion. The women's queue, I should add. All the men were around the back pissing on the hydrangeas under the tank stand.

The toilet routine was fascinating. All those polite kindergarten mothers not bothering to shut the door. Lots of dress flouncing, toilet paper bunching and laughter. Quite an education for young

Richard. I remember one noisy woman calling out to Dad, back at his station by the keg, 'Dick! Come and give me a hand!' And Dad shouting back, 'Shut up, Shirley!'

I'd wake up in the morning to the sound of clinking bottles and vacuum cleaning. Two more fancy red lightshades broken in the living room 'chandelier' by Reg Timms' broomstick 'taiaha dance'. I don't remember that light fixture ever having a full set of matching shades.

Minimum fuss, minimum aftermath. Did they clean up before they went off into the night? Probably. What looked like mayhem in the night looked like business as usual in the morning, except for old Jock Morrison asleep on the porch steps. Dad would be dragging him off over the road in a minute, in time to sweep up and get things ready for the morning homebrew session. Mum singing in the kitchen as she got the Sunday roast ready. Me at the dining table with my cornflakes.

I have no idea where my sisters were.

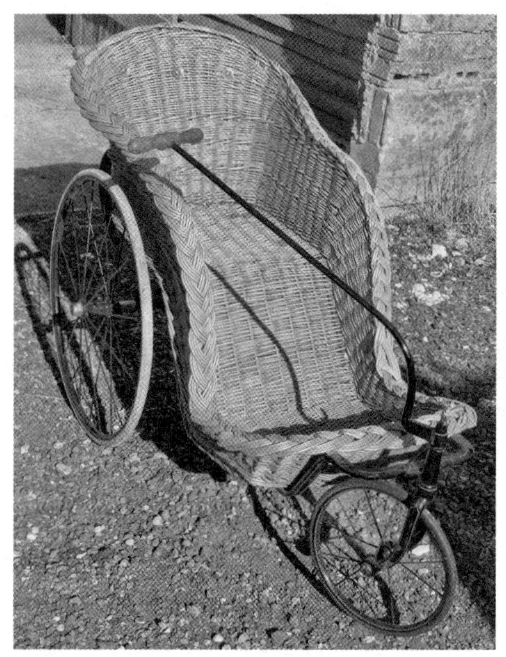

Hell on wheels.

14

I GOT A GUTS ACHE

I must have been about 13 and I knew what a stomach ache was, but this was a good one. It started out fine, like one of those day-off-school jobs where Mum fussed about with cold flannels and cod-liver oil and, once, Dad brought some comics home after work.

The comics were a surprise. I wasn't sure that Dad even knew what a comic was but he turned up at the end of my bed one afternoon with a *Phantom*, a *Mandrake* and another weird landscape-formatted thing called *The Bosun and Choclit*. Given Dad's dire warnings about bosuns, I was taken aback by this and even more intrigued by the bosun's sidekick, Choclit, a caricature of a little black boy with cornrows like rivets on his circular head, enormous wide-open eyes and big brown boots. Of course, back in the early 1950s no one knew what a stereotype was, nor that depicting cheeky little black fellows eating watermelons was a bad thing.

In Hastings, New Zealand we hardly knew what a black person was, but these bizarre portrayals, with their banjos, boots, battered top hats and grotesquely exaggerated lips, were everywhere: *Boy's Own Paper*, Cole's Book Arcade books, all the English 'funnies'. It's mind-boggling now to contemplate how ubiquitous and normalised these images were.

And then there were all the Chinese cooks and crooks with their teeth and pigtails. In *Blackhawk*, a war comic featuring a swash-buckling band of mercenaries working to save America, the multinational group featured a huge-chinned Swede, a rakishly moustachioed Frenchman and a faithful Chinese sidekick complete with the teeth, pigtail and a cleaver. His name, believe it or not, was Chop-chop. He didn't even get to wear the faintly fascist brass band uniform of the other members of the team, but had to settle for a mad ensemble of lurid green and yellow rags. I loved that crazy comic.

But nothing was going to divert me from *this* stomach ache. It seemed to go from ache to stabbing pain in about five minutes, causing me to sit bolt upright in bed and scream in agony, shedding comic books and flannels like autumn leaves. Mum bundled me into the Austin and rushed up St Aubyn Street to Dr Mitchell's rooms, where he did that flat-fingered pushing-down thing on my delicate abdomen, frowning deeply all the while, before looking across my recumbent dressing-gowned form and saying to Mum, 'This boy's appendix has burst and you must get him to the hospital immediately!'

What a fearful trip that was — Mum grimly gripping the

steering wheel and hurtling over the railway lines, down through Stortford Lodge (not a fishing resort) and up and into the Hastings Hospital turn-around, on two wheels.

I was whisked away — everyone gets whisked away in hospitals, don't they?

I remember lying on a rolling bed thing in a corridor somewhere and a nurse giving me something to calm me down. I fought against the stupor that threatened to overwhelm me because I thought that if I went to sleep I'd wake up when the knife went in.

And I did wake up, in the same corridor and the same bed. They'd forgotten me. In a panic I called out to a passing nurse, 'Nurse, nurse! If they don't operate on me soon I'll die!' She came over and said, 'It's OK, Richard, they've done it. The operation is over. Would you like a drink of water?' And she offered me an odd-looking teapot device with a spout and no handle which she fed into my misbehaving mouth; water went everywhere. I was still burbling when I reached down and felt a huge padded cummerbund thing around my middle.

After a spell they wheeled me into what I guess was a post-op recovery room, lined with monitors, looped tubes and cables, and left me there. I thought it was over, done — appendix, burst or otherwise, out; time to go home. So I swung my legs over the side of the gurney and stood up. Well, that was the plan, but my legs hadn't been informed and they folded up under me like wet noodles as I collapsed onto the lino in a deflating pile of pyjamas and plaid dressing gown. I lay there marvelling at the miscommunication between head and legs until someone came by and got me back onto the trolley.

After a bit of stern finger-wagging I was wheeled off down the corridor, feeling rather sorry for myself, until we arrived at a large room full of men, old men. A bit spooky, I thought, but we kept on wheeling right down the room, between the beds and out the other end into a small sunporch surrounded by windows and containing four beds. Grown-up men were propped up in three of them, and a bewildered but happy-to-be-alive 13-year-old was soon propped up in the fourth. Apparently the children's ward was full, so there I was.

And what a fabulous bit of serendipity that turned out to be. Like Chop-chop in the Blackhawks I became a sort of mascot: the butt of plenty of good-natured ribbing and the focus of an odd amount of pride as my stay progressed. Because Hastings was so small, everyone seemed to know someone who knew someone and it was never long before the adults would be swapping tales about mutual acquaintances. I loved the camaraderie.

In the corner opposite me was Blackhawk #1, a dashing Errol Flynn type of guy called Terry Schofield. (*Terry and the Pirates*, another comic book favourite. You can see how I was starting to appreciate my situation.) Terry had lost a leg above the knee in a top-dressing accident: he'd hooked the undercarriage of his Cessna in a fence on his landing approach. Always cheerful, he seemed to think it was a bit of an adventure. He showed me the stump one day and I was impressed with the way they'd made a clever flap of skin below the wound so it could be folded back up over the sawn-off stump and stitched in place.

The bed next to me was occupied by Angus Gordon, one of those hearty Hawke's Bay farmer types who'd had an unfortunate bit of bounce-back with a chainsaw. But even with half his head in bandages he seemed remarkably sanguine about his circumstances. Talking was a bit of a challenge but it didn't slow him down much. He told me that he was going to be a writer when he was 'finished with herding sheep'. 'Angus Gordon,' he said. 'Remember that name.'

To my fascination, he seemed to know all the nurses personally, and he also introduced me to marmalade, something that never featured in our house. The orderlies would bring it around in a large tin with the word 'OAK' printed boldly on the label. More emulsified than is fashionable nowadays, and no doubt full of sugar, it was scooped out of the tin like a stiff, lumpy jelly. I loved it. 'Where's Richard's marmalade ration?' Angus would loudly and half-intelligibly declare.

The last bed was on rotate: you'd wake up with a new roommate every second or third day or so. One day the bed was occupied by a grumpy old bugger called Bill McKenzie. His mates visited him in groups of six or seven, and they'd pull the curtains — no one else ever pulled the curtains — which would kick and flap like a dog-fight under a fat lady's skirts, all to the inimitable sound of uncapped hip flasks. Bill was always in a much better mood after the visits.

One day Alec Hamilton turned up in the bed; he'd lost a testicle in a rugby match. He worked for Dad in the engine room at Tomoana, greasing and oiling the machinery. I was familiar with the machines he referred to — the valves, dials and condensers that looked like the inside of Jules Verne's submarine, every spigot and pulley driven by a monstrous cast-iron fly-wheel so big that only half of it appeared above the floor. Half a dozen or so belts ran off the drum to disappear down into a deep trench, then reappear back up to their individual rims on the great wheel.

It never stopped, its main job to drive all the compressors that sent the ammonia on its never-ending gaseous circuit around all the freezers. All that fantastic palaver — from the shepherds, to the slaughtermen, to the varsity students sorting through the guts, to the colour-blind loco driver and our new patient oiling the widgets — was solely about freezing lamb for the Smithfield markets in London.

Because Alec knew Dad in a professional boss–worker relationship, he could tell me stories about how particular Dad was about his engine room. Everything had to be constantly spick and span. The hooter had to be blown on the dot. He even marvelled at Dad's tight capitalised script, a legacy of writing in the ship's log. Funny to be hearing about your dad as if he was just another person in the world.

So that was our little world. I felt like some sort of privileged POW, with my three fellow bed-bound survivors.

Apart from the big stitched wound in my lower right abdomen I felt perfectly fine. The only real discomfort came when the draining tube had to be pulled forth and shortened a smidge once a day. More a piece of latex pleated lengthwise, which protruded from the belly-button end of the wound, this was draining all the poison from the burst appendix. The muck and the mess round the opening would form a sort of crust that had to be broken every time the bloody thing was due for an abbreviation. Not a lot of fun. But once that little procedure had been attended to I was free to do as I pleased. So I explored.

One day I found an old-fashioned wheelchair at the back of a room full of discarded equipment. It was like an elongated cane armchair with two big wheels at the rear and one medium-sized wheel in the front, steered by a tiller. The best bit of all was the means of propulsion. A chain, like a bike chain, ran up from a sprocket on one of the big rear wheels to a larger sprocket mounted to the right of where the arm of the chair would have been. You sat back in the depths of the chair, holding the tiller with your left hand, while reaching up with your right hand to grab the jack handle that cranked the top sprocket. Having managed to extract this antique, I quickly became a marauding force in the silent and polished corridors of the hospital.

No one seemed to care where I went. In my dressing gown and pyjamas I got to know every ramp in the complex, flying further and further afield until one day I found myself way out the back by the morgue and the big, industrial-looking incinerator. What fresh hell went on back there? The incinerator was doing a mighty job: I suspect that's where Terry's leg went. On one visit I witnessed a body being ferried from an ambulance into the morgue. I once peered in the door at all the suspicious-looking benches. I used to call in on my rounds, greeting the orderlies sitting in the sun eating their tomato sandwiches as I flashed past, taking the corner on two wheels and getting out at the steepest ramps to give it a push.

I got totally lost once and found myself in what must have been the children's ward, where I should have been. It was a big, long room full of patients who, to my eyes, seemed as if they had suddenly shrunk. Quite odd. I didn't linger. I didn't belong there; I was a Blackhawk.

One day Mum brought me a pile of art materials. I've written about this before, the magic of the pencil, but it bears repeating. It still amazes me when people discover that you can make a bunch of lines on a bit of paper look like something. Once the word got around that I could draw, the nurses all wanted pictures of horses, lots of horses, which are a hell of a thing to draw from memory. I faked it for a spell, hiding the fetlocks in long grass and only drawing the damned animals in profile. I didn't even know that horses had shoulders, let alone those counter-intuitive hind legs where everything seems to bend the wrong way.

My bluffing and fudging was starting to wear a bit thin, until one of the nurses brought in quite specific photographs of her horse, including one of the animal jumping a hurdle from the front in three-quarter view. This dramatic image became one of my star turns. No one seemed to notice that it was always the same horse. To break things up a bit, I would sometimes flip the tracing and have the beast leaping from the left. Changing the nature of the jump itself, from rails to hedge, was another good trick.

I wonder where all those drawings are now. The recipient always seemed to carry the finished rendering away as if it had come from the tireless coloured pencils of Rex the Wonder Artist, who bashed out three-minute portrait sketches at the Easter Show. He drew on a pre-signed tablet of foolscap sheets, then, on completion of the portrait, he'd whisk in a border round the edge, the pencil gripped flat in his fist, the protruding thumb guiding the depth of the margin. In my memory, and I watched a lot, all his subjects ended up looking pretty much the same. Needless to say, I wasn't about to memorialise any of my nurses with a portrait. I knew my limits: Mickey Mouse, Donald Duck and horses.

Eventually my adventures as a pyjama-clad nabob drew to a close. The incremental cutting of the drain tube was counting down the days for me. On about the thirteenth day it was decided that its job was done and that the entire thing could be removed. I assumed the procedure would be a doddle, but the damn thing seemed to emerge forever. I could feel it unwinding inside me as the nurse gently pulled on the end until, with a wet sort of *floop*, it popped out and dangled from the forceps like an exhausted tapeworm. I had a couple more days of observation, and one day for the bloody great wool-bale stitching to be removed, and I was ready to be discharged.

But the night before I was due to leave something truly wonderful happened: the nurses were going to a ball. They'd been talking about it for days: who was going to be there, what they were going to wear, their hairdos. My team of Blackhawks teased them about it mercilessly — 'If I wasn't lying here with one leg!' Such was the excitement that we all began to imagine we were somehow going too.

Then, on the night, three of our favourite nurses crept into our cosy little annex and gave the four of us a special preview of their gowns. Rustling and giggling, they turned on the soft ceiling light in the middle of the room and, one by one, did a cute little twirl in the small space between the ends of the four beds. We watched, enthralled. And then they left, still giggling and rustling.

I left the next day. Sirens blared, sprinklers arched over the driveway, a brass band played, the entire hospital personnel waved from every vantage point and angels sang as the streamer-festooned Austin made its way majestically out onto the main road. I sat in the back, clutching a small tin of Oak marmalade.

All the fun of the fair.

15

GREAT BALLS OF FIRE!

I didn't know I could eat so much sweetcorn. I mean, we ate a lot of corn back at our place — a couple of cobs on the plate — but this was something else.

I was a guest for lunch at a market garden on the edge of town. The hearty folk who owned the place grew corn. Lots of corn. The cornfields started almost at the back door and seemed to stretch as far as my low sightline could see. Maybe it was maize — I never could tell the difference — but the cobs heaped up on a platter in the middle of the congoleum tablecloth were definitely sweetcorn.

'Help yourself, Richard,' said Mr D'Arth as I sat back after my normal two. I ate corn until I couldn't eat corn. My new friend Bruce (and the reason I was out there) sat there looking at me in amazement, as if he'd never seen a boy eat corn before.

And he probably hadn't. Bruce was down from Auckland to stay with his grandparents. Exotic, faraway Auckland. He was the son of one of Mum's best friends from the old days, when they worked and played together as single girls up in the big smoke. She was one of those old friends you call 'Aunty', Aunty Elsie, which didn't make Bruce my cousin, but did oblige us to assume that we'd at least be friends.

Bruce was a year older than me, at an age when a year conferred massive seniority on a chap, but fortunately he didn't seem the slightest bit inclined to take advantage of the gap. And this worked for me because I was very struck by this suave Aucklander with his assured air and cosmopolitan manner. He spoke like a detective from a paperback novel: teeth together, mouth to one side, lips pursed and even a hint of his R's being pronounced as W's, which somehow sounded oddly cool.

Even being out of his element didn't seem to faze him. When we were allowed to take turns on the tractor and plough, I foolishly thought that this was my time to shine. I clutched the big flat wheel with grim determination, my head craned uncomfortably around to keep the whole operation lined up as perfectly as possible, but Bruce went at it as if he'd been doing it all his life — body half turned in the metal bucket seat, one hand on the wheel and the other resting casually on the lip of the massive mudguard.

As a result of all this bonding I was allowed to go up to Auckland in the next school holidays, to stay with Aunty Elsie.

Gorgeous Aunty Elsie. I think I had a crush on her, if I'd known what that was. With her red lipstick, cigarettes and long, swishy, calf-length cotton print frocks, she was the most glamorous thing I'd ever seen. I could've just hung around the little Dean Street villa in Arch Hill all day, chatting to her about the old days with Mum, while she waved her red nails in the air, chuckling her smoker's chuckle. Bruce wasn't very much in evidence. I think he had a girlfriend, while I still had khaki shorts and sandals.

But I couldn't sit around all day gazing at Bruce's mum, and I did manage to get out of the house on one spectacular occasion. Mum had decided that 'while I was up there' I should pop up and see an obscure relation of hers who lived in Browns Bay. I think she must have forgotten how spread out Auckland was, even back then, before the bridge. Going to Browns Bay was like going to the Bay of Islands.

I got up there OK. Elsie packed my school bag and sent me off with instructions for the ferry, bus and relatives. I walked down to the terminal, caught the ferry, bussed up to Browns Bay and somehow found the house — a buttercup yellow Art Deco place up a sunny pathway lined with rose bushes. I went in, said hello to these complete strangers, had an orange cordial, looked at the sea view from the lounge window, then turned around and did the whole thing in reverse. This time the ferry crossing was quite rough, with lots of rocking and rolling — tough on the old people, fun for me.

It was dusk by the time we pulled into the downtown terminal and I decided to treat myself to another cordial at a small kerbside pie cart opposite the Ferry Building before hoofing it off up Queen Street. I was standing there in my shorts and sandals drinking my cordial right next to an extremely drunk individual who was leaning forward, face down, on the pie cart counter. As I knocked the last of my drink back I felt rain splash on my sandalled feet and I cast an anxious eye skyward from under the awning. Except that it wasn't rain. My counter chum was pissing directly into the gutter at our feet. I dropped the glass and leapt backwards. This was turning into a long day.

I continued my odyssey up Queen Street but halfway up, for some reason, I turned off, thinking it would be a short cut up to Arch Hill, then made my way north again at what would've been Albert Street. It was all residential back then — rows of verandahed workers' cottages. And this was where it all got a bit *Pilgrim's Progress*.

My first bizarre encounter was with a large Pasifika gentleman, wearing a singlet, football shorts and sandals, stumbling/walking towards me with a massive turban-like bandage on his head. I was hypnotised by the sight. As he grew parallel to me he stopped, raised a meaty hand in a cheerful salute and gave me a huge smile, revealing a mouthful of teeth, all covered in blood. There was plenty of blood elsewhere — rivulets of it trickling down his temple from under the bandage. He stood there swaying a bit, giving me plenty of time to inspect him under the streetlight, before proceeding in his odd staggering, swaggering way.

Heart-rate up, I continued my journey but had only gone about a block when I saw, on the other side of the road, a skinny guy, stripped to the waist, hauling a distraught woman along the footpath. Feeling safe enough with the street between us, I stopped and shouted out as loudly as I could, 'Leave that woman alone!' Seriously, those were my actual words. The man was so surprised he let go of the woman and made to cross the street. His victim bolted, and so did I, my healthy young Hawke's Bay legs propelling me at great speed all the way up and over Great North Road to Aunty Elsie's front door.

'You won't believe what just happened to me!' I gasped to Bruce when he opened the door. And I don't think he did. But Aunty Elsie did, and thought it prudent that none of it got back to Mum or there would be no more holidays in Auckland. There definitely were more trips back to the big smoke. Before that, though, the revolution happened: rock'n'roll hit New Zealand.

It was a sunny day in Hastings in 1955 and I was skating on the concrete path that half-circled the big house at 507 when the sash window of the kitchen went up with a bang and Mum stuck her head out: 'Richard! Come in here! It's this new rock'n'roll!' I dutifully clomped into the kitchen in my skates — metal wheels on linoleum — and stood there listening to Bill Haley belt out 'Rock Around the Clock'. I wasn't very impressed. A song about clocks? What the hell was that all about? I liked my country and western 'story' songs. Two weeks later and I couldn't get enough of it.

Then two or three years later down came Bruce, and he was quite the heart throb. Draped coat and pegleg trousers, long black hair that he kept combing back like Elvis Presley in the opening scene of *King Creole*. Not a lot of corn eating and ploughing went on on this holiday. In fact Bruce and his younger brother Gerald hung out at our place in Hastings more than we did out at the D'Arths'. I recall Gerald creating a bit of a stir among my sisters, and I have a striking memory of Bruce playing the piano for Mum — Aunty Joan. Elsie must have asked him to, and he graciously obliged.

Bruce sat down quietly, flicked his hair back with a shake of his head and ripped straight into Jerry Lee Lewis's 'Great Balls of Fire'. He did the whole thing — leapt to his feet, kicked the piano stool back out of the way and went at it like a man possessed. I was agog. Mum didn't know whether to be shocked or excited and somehow settled on something in between: lots of throat clearing and apron flapping. It certainly put my 'North to Alaska' in the shade.

Bruce taught me a few left-hand boogie-woogie riffs, then buggered off back to Auckland. I'm surprised that Mum let me go back up there but the following year off I went. And everything had changed. It turned out that Bruce had a dad, a suave and roguish streak of handsome who'd left Elsie just before my last visit and was living with his new partner in a brand-new Californian bungalow on Dominion Road. The house is still there — all sleek levels, curtain glass, portholes and a flat-profile stone chimney. We went over there once, Bruce and I, and walked round on the shagpile carpet, into and out of the conversation pit.

I remember, too, the record he put on for us: 'Love Potion Number 9'. We knew what rock'n'roll was but this was different. Was it the crazy lyrics — the guy kisses a cop on Thirty-fourth and what, Vine? Or maybe I was mesmerised by the white carpet? I don't know. Maybe the environment made me feel I was actually in America, listening to American music. Maybe it was because it was played to us by a six-foot smoothie in pressed slacks and grey loafers. None of this was new to Bruce, of course, and I could see where he got the other 50 per cent of his style from.

I wasn't doing too badly with my flat top and Tony Curtis duck's arse but there was no way I was going to keep up with Bruce. Auckland was Bruce's town, Hastings was mine. And I felt it every time we went out. I especially remember a trip out to the Easter

Show, held in Western Springs back then. Bruce, naturally, brought along his gorgeous girlfriend. And my role seemed to be to keep the girlfriend's girlfriend entertained. Living dolls like Bruce's girl always seemed to team up with slightly lesser sidekicks who posed no threat to the alpha-girl's obvious supremacy.

So that's two sidekicks teamed up and following along like pet chihuahuas, sitting like stiffs behind them on the Big Wheel, watching Bruce's casual arm-around-the-shoulder action while we were too scared to even look at each other. It was 'excruciatin'', as my father used to say. Bruce knocked over the stacked Donald Duck blocks and loaded his girlfriend up with stuffed toys. I acquitted myself well at the shooting gallery, but I don't think my escort was even watching.

I could see my friendship with Bruce drifting away and my rapidly evolving fascination with art wasn't helping. In fact I did a special painting of a dead tree in the desert for Aunty Elsie as a thank you for staying with her. I wonder what Bruce made of that?

I don't think I ever went back to Dean Street again. I headed off south to art school; Bruce went on to play with various bands around Auckland. And that was pretty much it, until years later, when I was married and had moved up to Auckland. I ran into him, managing a machinery hire place out at Panmure. Mr Cool in a badly fitting white collar and tie, biros in his top pocket. I didn't see him again until he popped up in the media years later as the part-owner of the biggest trucking and logistics company in the history of New Zealand. Go figure.

Keep fingers and toes clear.

16

MOWING MOLLY'S LAWNS

As I've established, the Frizzells had Hastings covered. It was interesting that Molly was positioned in the centre of the family web because I suspect that a lot of powerful signals emanated from her trim bungalow, and also interesting that Nora had elected to position herself as far away as possible, out on the edge of the loop. I was never quite sure of the dynamic — what can an 11- or 12-year-old pick up of these grown-up things? — but there was definitely something going on.

Dad was obviously under some sort of obligation to Molly because of the mortgage that bought the fabulous old pile on Sylvan Road, which came with Molly's cast-off 1930s Austin Ten-Four Sherborne. It was a quiet duty, nothing too onerous, but certain rituals and behaviours had to be adhered to. Molly was

Presbyterian through and through and it didn't take much to get her clutching her wattles. I don't remember either of the sisters ever setting foot in our house, as if it was some sort of den of iniquity and too damn bohemian altogether with Mum's mad craft efforts all over the walls and the equally unruly kids running wild. Dad's rip, shit and bust approach to gardening wouldn't have impressed them much either.

Despite his landscaping lapses, one of Dad's duties was mowing Molly's lawns, and when I was deemed old enough, it became one of mine. Early in the piece — before Molly lashed out and bought a new mower — we had to take the old Morrison back and forth in the boot of the Austin. This was quite a performance. Because the boot opened out like an oven door, Dad had to heave the entire machine up and lodge it into the shallow V shape thus created, and strap it down. Then he'd unload it at his sister's place, about six or seven blocks up the road, leave me to it and come back later to reload the steaming beast for the return home. I'd be waiting in the incredibly spick and span kitchen, perched at the Formica table drinking blackcurrant cordial out of a very tall, faceted glass.

Mowing Molly's lawns was always an exercise in precision — none of that full-steam-ahead barging about that took place at 507. Molly liked her lawns mowed, not ploughed. She was also a very serious gardener and everything had to be just so. No regurgitated clumps from a too-full catcher and no accidental pruning of the herbaceous borders. I had to mow next to these armed with a stick, so that I could reach forward and raise the drooping floral fringe up out of the way of the rollers and the spinning blades, all the while watching that the front guide-wheels didn't stray off the carefully spaded lawn edge, causing the mower to grind out a nice little exit-ramp from lawn to garden. Because the Morrison was one of those old self-drive mowers with a big driving roller at the back, throttling, steering and deploying my stick simultaneously was quite an art.

When the catcher showed signs of reaching full capacity — when the first errant clump hit the skids — and because Molly didn't like the mower left idling as you wandered off with the catcher because it left a mark, you had to time your circuit to end up at the enormous compost bins situated over in the work area of the property. This was a sort of hidden corner where a certain degree of healthy gardening chaos was allowed to occur. Tucked back in under a spreading oak tree were potting benches, piles of terracotta pots, bundles of stakes, large framed wire netting dirt sieves and the collapsing remains of an old chook-house and run. And those mighty bins, one doing the rotting down and the other one building up to it. I suspect Dad might have had a hand in their construction, given the degree of overreach on the scale. It was all I could do to heave the catcher over the top rail to tip in the clippings.

I think a lot of my romantic dreams about how to garden were impressed upon me by that corner — the dirt underfoot, the ordered disorder. When we played hide and seek on the annual Christmas Day visit I'd hide way behind the collapsing chook-house, knowing that not even my adventurous Pākōwhai Road cousins would venture that far back into the cobwebby cave.

The garden had to be really looking its best for the Christmas party. It was quite a ritual. In fact the whole day was rituals all the way.

The day began at home of course, with the usual rush of excitement early in the morning with the opening of the presents — more Hornby trains or Meccano for me.

After tearing everything apart and putting it aside for later, and putting the orange from the toe of the stocking back in the fruit bowl, we'd all sit down to Christmas dinner — at lunchtime.

With only a couple of hours to recover from that blowout we'd all scrub up and drive up to Aunty Molly's for afternoon tea. All the cousins converged for this one. Uncle George, Aunty Cath and their rowdy brood from the market garden to the north. The 'bookish' lot from the south thrown together with their rural cousins, or the 'horsey' lot, as we came to know them, because there always seemed to be a horse somewhere in the gardens, either down among the berry vines or stabled at the end of the packing shed.

My earliest recall of the Aunty Molly royal garden party is a strange one — right on the edge of my memory, like a vivid viewfinder flash. The snapshot is of the great Frizzell matriarch, mother of Molly, Nora, George and Dick, former laundry mistress of Waikoko House at Tomoana, sitting erect in a chair out in the middle of the lawn with all her black skirts and ruffles spread out around her like those statues of Queen Victoria you see everywhere. All in black from head — mantilla even — to invisible toe, motionless, as everyone else milled about her like chickens around a very aloof mother hen. Just that one image and she was gone. It was a sunlit glimpse into Dad's mysterious past. Oh, he *did* have a mother.

Afternoon tea was served on the front porch, the special one. I loved that porch, so different from the long colonial verandahs at home. It was really a large square outside room with long squabs on three sides running underneath heavy shallow concrete arches with striped awnings that could be rolled up or down with a rope and pulley arrangement depending on the angle of the sun. A set of concrete steps flowed in a short, wide sweep down to the 'big lawn' — the one I carefully patterned in parallel stripes of pale and dark green.

You could, if you were brave enough, get to the porch *through the house.* From the spotless kitchen with its large black and white floor tiles — I used to pretend that the black ones were the tops of huge pillars going miles down to the misty valley floor represented by the white ones — you would creep up the hallowed hall past the very shut bedroom doors and into the mysterious front lounge, a room of no use at all except, weirdly enough, for a large, wooden kind of pachinko board set up flat on the carpet. It was like a varnished plywood pinball field with lots of little nail fences clustered here and there around which the ball bearings poinged once sent on their way with a sprung flick of a little piston down in the right-hand corner. What was it doing there? It looked as if you could have way more fun with it than could possibly be allowed in this hushed, blinds-half-drawn Presbyterian environment.

Just as my poor parched father's tongue was about to hit the floor, we'd all pile back into the cars and drive over to Aunty Nora's for her turn at the Christmas hospitality ritual. Nora didn't come to Molly's because she was busy setting up for round three, and Molly didn't come to Nora's because she had to tidy up. Did they ever do anything together?

After the formality of the Molly experience, Aunty Nora's was like being let out of school. Walking on the beach, picking up coal, running up to the sunroom to 'view Bay View', eating sausage rolls and banana cake in the beachy kitchen and drinking fizzy drink out of curly-topped bottles. And I loved her books. A whole shelf of higgledy-piggledy well-read volumes: *Snugglepot and Cuddlepie*, *The Magic Pudding*, Cole's Book Arcade . . . There was even a very early Peter McIntyre book, and you can imagine how much I loved leafing through that.

And no formal garden — no lawn — just gravel, rock gardens and concrete-slab crazy paving planted about with succulents and hardy coastal plants like ngaio and rock daisies. Aunty Nora would stride about showing us her latest bit of tamed wilderness and telling her brother what to do and how she needed him to get someone to look at her septic tank.

Her whole set-up, and the mad sea with its awesome undertow, felt so robust and windswept, so different from Molly's flower beds. I don't think, either, that Nora cared so much for the church, and I've always been of the opinion that this aunt, with her beach house, trousers and steel grey plait, was more tolerant than Molly, but my sisters tell me otherwise. It seems she could be as disapproving of certain modern mores as her sister. Perhaps I was impressed with her mannish ways, her loud, 'C'mon Richard, eat up!', as if we were both on the same wavelength.

So that was the Aunty Molly and the Aunty Nora rituals done for another Christmas, all in one day. (We did, though, repeat the Nora one occasionally throughout the year, Dad slipping off down the beach for a top-up from his hip flask — what his sister called his little 'boozy-doozy'.) Off we'd drive, all the way back through Napier, Clive, past the showgrounds and back home, too knackered to play with our presents.

On Boxing Day I had to bike back up to Molly's and help with the restoration as she huffed and puffed over what had been broken or flattened in the cousins' boisterous crashing about. I never minded: it was sunny, the garden fascinated me. I was happy to be there, and Aunty Molly seemed happy to have me there playing gardener.

Because it wasn't all about lawn mowing. There were always lots of chores lined up for me to attend to: raking and barrowing leaves and rotting fruit, putting all the lawn furniture back where it was before I moved it to mow, trimming all the path edges with that rolling blade thing. Rather a satisfying chore that last one — rumbling up the footpath, slicing through the encroaching couch grass, reducing it to a military trim. Prunings to gather and a perpetually smouldering incinerator to be kept topped up. And like a good general, Molly would be out there with me somewhere, keeping me moving, making the most of my visit.

She wasn't a large woman, quite small in fact, with a head of pure white hair halo-ing her face, but she had a large presence. I don't know if it was something she'd had to assume as the family anchor after her father's untimely demise, or a natural older sister thing, but she sure knew how to direct traffic. And this barely reigned-in imperiousness was aided to some degree by her physical bearing.

Like most of the matrons who patronised her shop — 'M. Frizzell', read the sign — Aunty Molly had a very impressive bosom. As she was down on her hands and knees on the lawn, trowelling away at one of her flowering borders, I'd be called forward for another directive. I'd be standing opposite her on the path, on the other side of the narrow garden being attended to, looking directly down the valley of her mighty cleavage.

She could have sat back on her haunches to deliver the instructions but she would stay on gloved hands and knees throughout. I don't know if she'd loosened her stays or whatever because of the hot Hawke's Bay day, but there was a lot of bosom trying to get out of that sunfrock (from her shop, no doubt). I couldn't take my eyes off this titanic battle between gravity and unbound cotton.

I know, it's starting to sound like an Alberto Moravia novel and I often wondered if she was having me on in an impish Molly way — blue eyes looking innocently up at me over her rimless spectacles as this great display of matronly mammaries swayed beneath her.

I'd be in such a state that I could hardly retain whatever it was she was trying to explain to me. Then I'd spend the rest of my visit awaiting further instruction.

I never thought I'd ever be recording that, but there it is, Molly and me, out in the garden, drunk with pollen and birdsong.

The walnut Hilton.

17

TUNNELLING OUT OF HASTINGS

I couldn't have pictured a more perfect playground if I'd been asked to design one from scratch. It looked like an art-directed set-up for a BNZ ad.

The big in-and-out driveway snaking round between the walnut tree, the old garage, the big gumtree stump and the woodshed. The sun filtering down into a cleared space beneath the huge tree where the swing hung down in a pool of light. The magic kingdom counter-balanced by a very vertical rimu that brushed the outer edge of the walnut tree's crown. The ground around the swing clearing carpeted with wild irises and rotting walnuts.

This was my domain. Not exclusively mine, because my sisters used to play on the swing, cook chips on the secret fireplace in the gap between the gumtree stump and the neighbour's fence and play leaping games off the top of the stump down into the flax bushes that fringed it. But it felt like mine. In my head I ruled over it, wrote policy, issued permits, held sway.

Whatever I was up to, especially in the weekend, Dad was never far away, either digging in his garden, planting more potatoes, turning the great landmass that was his compost heap (frustratingly close to the trunk of 'my' walnut tree) or clattering around in the garage. The mighty garage.

The story was that 507 Sylvan Road used to be some sort of inn and the coach horses would overnight in the garage — and it did seem to have a row of horse manger-ish bins along the back wall. It sounds like complete nonsense when I think about it now, but who knows: it was a very big shed. The huge bifold doors were covered with green and cream paint where Dad used to work out his house painting brushes with turps before washing them in warm, soapy water.

Behind the permanently folded back doors on the left, facing the shed, Dad kept the sacks of potatoes in lime that he harvested from the spare section. One of my regular chores was getting out enough potatoes for dinner and washing the lime off them. Behind the other great colonial portal he kept all his gardening tools: hoes, rakes, shovels, all lined up with deep holes drilled down into the tops of their wooden handles that he kept full of engine oil as they wintered over. Woe betide anyone who messed with *those* noble implements.

All manner of junk was stored in the generous spaces up and down either side of the garage — you could've just about got two cars in there side by side with room to spare — including a large sideboard on the left full of homebrew that occasionally exploded in storage. On the right-hand side, looking out onto the curving driveway, were towering mullioned windows filtering the light through their grimy, rippling panes onto the workbench.

But before we go into the story of the workbench I'll try and explain Dad's venetian-blind-painting apparatus, which occupied the space between the bench and the garden tools. Every window in the big house had wooden venetians and they seemed to need constant upkeep. It was like painting the Auckland Harbour Bridge: you got to the end and then had to start again at the beginning with the retaping, re-cording and painting. Hawthorn Green, I think it was called.

Dad had fixed up a system: a V-shaped wooden thing like a chook-feeding trough the full length of a venetian blind slat. He would lay one slat flat in the V, paint it, turn it over with a practised flick using two paint-stiffened freezing works mittens to hold it open-palmed at either end, and paint the other side. Then, still with the open-palmed mittens, he would pick it up by either end and hang it on a nail, in a row of nails that could accommodate an entire venetian blind. Swipe, swipe, turn, swipe, swipe, hang, and there was a whole deconstructed venetian blind hanging there drying out. Genius. Then the brush would be banged out, slap, slap, on the garage doors and put in a tin of turps for tomorrow.

Now, moving right along the wall to the workbench. But what's that underneath? A big black box full of tools: ballpeen hammers (because he was an engineer, not a carpenter), hacksaws, hundreds of broken hacksaw blades (good for fixing the spark plug gap on the lawn mower), pliers, wrenches, cold chisels, spanners of every size and weight, soldering irons — and files, lots and lots of files. Not rasps — they're for wood — but those useless metal files with very small teeth. Why so many? Were they just easy to accidentally walk away with, stuck in the hip pocket of your overalls? I used to think that if I burrowed down deep enough I'd find some sign of Dad's young life as an apprentice engineer at Niven's Engineering Workshops in Napier. I did find a nifty piece of gear once: a Jules Verne-style measuring device with a sliding scribe and adjustable thumbscrew. Mostly, though, it was files.

The workbench — what a thing of wonder it was, scarred with saw cuts, and chisel notches, stained black with oil and paint, gouged and pitted, embossed with the tacks, staples and flathead rivets that us kids used to bang into it. It was probably about 9 feet long, with a dirty great engineer's vice at the end nearest the doors, the other end disappearing beneath a great avalanche of paint rags, paint and engine oil tins and pickle jars of various fluids: soldering flux, weedkiller, brake fluid, paint thinners and God knows what else. I suspect Dad didn't even know. I played mad scientist with the mystery contents — I'd pour different combinations from the unlabelled bottles into my lead-nail smelting saucepan and boil the mixture on one of my secret fireplaces. Oh, the foam and the fumes. I'm lucky I didn't blow myself up.

The vice was a handy implement. Good for crushing things. Good for holding lead-head nails in place while you tore the heads off for future smelting. Good for gripping live .303 rounds while you pliered the bullet bit away from the gunpowder bit.

I actually did this once. A bit jealous of Gavin's polished-up memento from the fish in a barrel experiment, I decided to make one of my own. I rummaged around in Dad's bedside drawer and found a .303 shell jumbled up with mismatched cufflinks, loose .22 bullets, old combs, silver hairbrushes, pocket knives and other male detritus.

I took the bullet — he'd never miss it — down to the garage, put it in the vice, twisted and tugged the actual bullet (the pointy end) out and poured out the gunpowder, which fascinated me because it came out in the form of slender rods, like sections of pencil lead. The plan was obviously to render the bullet harmless then jam the nose-cone back in, drill a hole through the back end, polish it up and wear it on a string round my neck. But first I wanted to make the shell look fired, 'authentic', and to that end I put the empty shell nose down in the vice, grabbed a handy 6-inch nail, placed it carefully in the centre of the small round bullseye at the arse end of the bullet, where the firing pin strikes it, and gave it a good whack with the ballpeen hammer.

What I didn't know about was the detonator, the thing that explodes and ignites the gunpowder, which then *really* explodes and sends the bullet on its way. The explosion in the garage was tremendous. I was shocked rigid, my hearing went, there was smoke everywhere, the place reeked of gunpowder. Mum came out of the kitchen onto the back steps, fortunately about 25 yards away, and through the settling fug I faintly heard her shout, 'Richard, what was that?' I hoarsely replied with some vague story about dropping the cast-iron boot-last onto the floor. She seemed to buy it and went back into the house. I slowly came to, relived it all in slow motion: the hammer coming down onto the nail, the great jet of flame shooting out of the bottom of the vice directly to the floor boards . . .

And now, with my bullet not around my neck because I could

never explain it, we leave the garage, go down its concrete apron, cross over the drive and approach the walnut tree. The noble walnut tree. Man, that tree could take it. The number of nails we hammered into it, the tomahawked notches and scarfs — it's a wonder it didn't curl up and die. But the tree refused to succumb and continued to fruit crazily every year.

It was the perfect hut tree.

I initiated it, but Dad quickly took over from my puny efforts. He even got his mates to come around to help him. The platform itself was a massive piece of engineering: huge beams notched into the living tree, just above the point where the trunk branched out into the beginning of the crown. With the platform completed and a trapdoor installed so you could get up onto it from below, it was time to concentrate on the actual hut. No ad hoc mucking about with salvaged lumber for these boys — men behaving like boys. They managed to somehow haul an entire piano crate up into the tree. As it slowly edged up into the leaves with the men hauling on the ropes, it looked enormous.

Anchored just south of the trapdoor, we cut a hinged door into the northern wall and a window into the side looking straight down to the driveway below. The last thing to go on was a stumpy lean-to corrugated iron roof that projected out the front just far enough to give a sense of a verandah. We hung the curtains, laid the lino and, bingo, a hut in a tree.

Once it was done, I don't think Dad showed any further interest in it. All I had to worry about was keeping my sisters out. Fortunately, with one exception, they didn't seem to be all that excited after the initial royal tour. I have to say, though, that there wasn't much room in there. Three or, at a pinch, four 11-year-old boys crammed together with their knees up round their ears was just about it. But we did it, and forced ourselves to have fun, smoking our driftwood cigars that we got smouldering in one of the smelting fires below and carrying them up. If you could find a length, usually gathered from the beach out at Te Awanga, with the right porosity it made for quite a satisfactory puff. Good thing we didn't install an actual window in the window hole.

Leo somehow managed to get hold of a copy of the famous nude photograph of Marilyn Monroe, the one with an incredibly young-looking Marilyn lying stretched out sideways on a huge rippling satin sheet. I got roped into making copies of the thing for the team, and the hut was the perfect venue for my transcribing endeavours. I'd sit hunched up, laboriously copying the picture with my coloured pencils. It was amazing how quickly it became less and less erotic as I persevered. It wasn't really that erotic to start with — only one pink breast on display, and one rather large pink nipple and a lot of sheet — but it still felt weird, rendering all those tones of pink. I kept the second one, the one where I got it more or less right and before standards started to slip.

I didn't know what to do with the one I kept — such hot, pink contraband. I couldn't pin it up in the hut — too many sisters — and so I folded it up into a Silver Fern tobacco tin and buried it in the rough garden by the garage where we kids tried to grow radishes for school projects. I buried it near the back, one pace out from the second window down from the woodshed. When I went back years later, there was nothing there, of course, not even a bit of rusty tin.

After my stint as a hut builder's apprentice I felt qualified to extend my domain vertically and I built a small platform seat, like an abbreviated Cape Cod chair, way up in the highest fork I could find that I figured would take the weight, and the nails. I had to haul the timber and the hammer up by rope. The nails went up in my pocket. I'd sit up there in glorious isolation, swaying in the breeze, reciting the wacky poems that Jack Porter taught me, or reading my *Just William* books.

With the space above ground conquered, I decided that it was time to tackle the space below it. The first underground hut was basically just a big pit with a tin roof covered in dirt. It was still rather effective, except that I hadn't thought to dig the rafters into the sides of the hole, which subsequently meant that the dirt roof looked like a Viking burial mound. No matter how much grass and weeds I planted on it, it was always very obviously there. The staired entry trench was a bit of a giveaway too. I'm not sure why I thought it had to be undetectable. I was probably thinking of all the Second World War escape accounts I was reading at the time — Colditz Castle secret tunnels under the coal stove and behind the latrine.

To that end I started to mine a tunnel inside the hut, into one of the dirt walls. This kind of worked for a few feet but was obviously too close to the surface. I hadn't dug the pit deep enough. Too easy for prison guards to detect. So I started a real one, a few yards from the mound, leaving the first attempt for my sisters to play in.

The new one took me months. First I dug a pit about 2 or 3 feet square (hard to say now because I'm a lot broader than I was then) straight down until it loomed satisfactorily over my head. Then, and this is the part that always amazes me, I went horizontal, towards the walnut tree, in the belief that the roots of the tree would act like tunnelling timbers. It worked. I kept this up for about the length of the vertical pit, using a hand trowel and a bucket on a rope to carry the spoil away to be distributed evenly over and around the diggings from the first hut. I built a 'secret' trapdoor to cover the entrance, adding more grass, dirt and weeds to camouflage my goings-on.

Once I'd progressed long enough horizontally to feel as though I'd gone somewhere, I slowly, by candlelight, opened the tunnel out into a space big enough for at least two of us to sit there with our knees up and experience the thrill of it all, and maybe refine it with a few more niches and nascent subsidiary tunnels. My tree root theory kicked in big time at this widening phase because I encountered quite a network, which I included as part of the subterranean architecture or chopped right out.

What did Mum think I was up to down there? Wasn't she at least a little worried? If she needed me for anything, like dinner, she'd lift up the secret lid/door (how did she know it was there?) and call down, 'Richard!' and I'd come crawling out. The beauty of the room was that you could turn around in it and come out head first, climbing up the shaft using the footholds provided.

When it was done, and all my mates had experienced it, it faded away as a destination of choice. It was a hell of a dirty business for a start — all that sticky yellow clay — and apart from the actual phenomenon it was all rather useless. You couldn't smoke driftwood down there, couldn't draw nude women, couldn't do anything really. I'd just made a hole. It needed to actually go somewhere — under the driveway, say, and up into the Langfords' primulas.

The first time I made it back home from art school I went down to the walnut tree to check it out. I lifted the lid, which by now really was starting to look like part of the landscape, to find my hole full of junk, with an old cast-iron toilet cistern lying right in the mouth. It was like Tutankhamun's tomb vandalised. Dad said that it had flooded, filled to the top with water — a scary prospect in anyone's backyard — and so he filled it in and had a big clean-up.

How forlorn I felt, standing there looking at the rusty cistern and down past it to a clay-clotted jumble of old bottles, jam jars and lots of files. I lowered the lid and went inside for a beer.

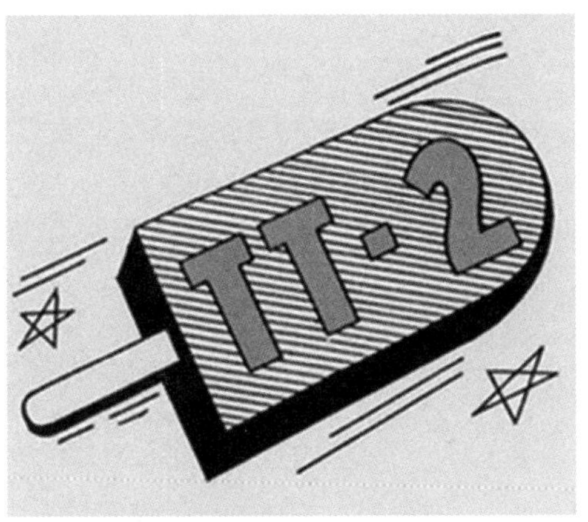

Excitement on a stick.

18

ROBINSON'S DAIRY

'Can you pop round to Robinson's dairy for me, Richard?' Mum would call from the kitchen. 'I need some frozen peas.' And I'd be on my bike like a shot and scooting off only a couple of blocks from our house. Robinson's Cash Store was on a corner site with the doors to the grocery on the Riverslea Road side and the dairy entrance on the St Aubyn Street side. There was an interior door in between; behind the back-to-back counters so staff could flit from shop to shop depending on the customer's location. You could ask for cheese in the grocery half and old Charlie Robinson or an employee could walk through to the dairy and chop you off a chunk. And I do mean 'chop' and 'chunk'.

There were only two varieties of cheese, cheddar and tasty, and both entire wheels sat out in plain sight on things like small butcher's blocks with an ominous wire connected to a T-shaped grip dangling from a strategic nail at the back. Depending on your preference the counter staff would grab the wire and garotte you off a wedge, wrap it up in greaseproof paper and off you went. Every time I went in there I'd be hoping for a bit of garrotting action.

One day, I was holding Mum's *Pix* magazine and a copy of *Truth* loosely in my arms eyeing up the latest *Uncle Scrooge* comic until the temptation overwhelmed me and I slipped it into the folds of the newspaper. I wanted it that badly. My pocket money was already spent, probably on *The Phantom*, so I just did it. Then, of course, I had to read it in secret and hide it under my mattress. And then, having finished with it, I returned it and slid it back on the shelf. I felt virtuous for a spell and did this twice before it dawned on me that I was doubling my chances of getting caught and began budgeting my pocket money more judiciously. It was a relief to read my comics without the imprint of the wire-wove distorting the text.

What a peculiar ritual the reading of the comic was. Because I didn't want my sisters reading over my shoulder(s), I read them in my bedroom. And because the room was so small, and my little work table always covered in drawing materials, I used to kneel at my bedside as if I was at prayer and lay the comic, especially those big *Century* compilations, before me on the bedspread, nice and flat, and read them like that. *Knockout* especially benefited from this system because it came in a loose-leaf unstapled tabloid form that could easily be muddled up if you didn't keep it carefully marshalled, or hidden from your sisters. This very British production also came from Robinson's and it was a big event when the day came round that I knew it'd be there, waiting for me.

On one such day Mum sent me off for a dozen sausages. I

bought them from the butcher, picked up my nice, fresh *Knockout*, put them both in Mum's string bag and slung it over the handlebars of my bike. I was pedalling merrily home when I must have taken the corner into Sylvan Road too dramatically. Centrifugal force, which isn't a real thing apparently but did the job on the day, sent the swaying bag into the space between the front forks and the spinning spokes of the wheel.

To say I ground to a halt pretty much describes the following action perfectly. Not so sudden that it pitched me over the handlebars, but definitely enough to let me know that something had gone dreadfully wrong. I was able to back-wind the front wheel and extricate the amorphous mess that used to be bag, sausages and comic. The sausages now appeared to be on the outside of the string bag, with my *Knockout* somehow distributed democratically through the great meaty wodge.

I meekly presented this bizarre package to Mum, holding it out by the still functioning handles in the faint hope that she would be able to disentangle it in her clever motherly way. She seemed to find the whole thing rather funny, and it must have been quite a sight: forlorn young Richard standing in the back door with his tragic offering. She quite cheerfully gave me money for another attempt and even supplemented the purse to the tune of a replacement *Knockout*.

After that she seemed to take quite a proprietary interest in my comic and even used to read some of the stories, particularly 'Our Ernie' (Dad's middle name was Ernest) with his, 'What's for tea, Ma?' catchcry. She became so annoyed with the loose binding that she took it upon herself to sew the comic together, running it through her trusty Singer as if she was hemming a skirt. I've still got them, my British comics with her meandering stitching going up and down just in front of the fold.

Close enough was always good enough for Mum — always bashing ahead in an excitable rush. One day when she nearly clipped the adjacent car going in for a tight angle park in front of the post office, I said, 'Wow, Mum, that was close!' and she replied, with an airy wave, 'An inch is as good as a mile.' I pondered on the meaning of that for months but it's fabulously true, isn't it?

Our little cosmopolitan nexus, the Parkvale CBD: chemist, draper, Robinson's, butcher and the fish and chip shop. The chemist didn't hold much interest for me until I started working there after school, and more on that later. The butcher I knew for his sausages. But the fish and chip shop was a different order of retail. They prepared stuff and sold it, and sometimes they sold the stuff untouched. Mum occasionally bought the unmade stuff, which she would bring home and utterly destroy in great baking dishes of milk left to simmer in the oven for hours. What was that all about? Taking a fish out of water and putting it in milk. Who dreamed that one up? Was it a British white on white thing?

Actually, it didn't stop with milky fish. For a special treat Mum would attempt homemade takeaway food: saveloys halved lengthwise, dipped in homemade batter and fried in the pan. Just like from the fish and chip shop . . . not.

I don't think she ever got the batter disgustingly heavy enough. She'd dip the half-sav in her watery mix, then transfer it, flat side down, to the pan, where the batter would drain off the recumbent form and fan out until it looked like a saveloy hiding under a thin pikelet, or even thinner, like a crepe with a frothy perimeter. And when she turned them over they seesawed on the almost batter-free spine of the sav like a flying saucer landing upside down in a puddle. We ate them, of course. It's hard to ruin a saveloy and they did have a certain charm — totally unrelated to the real thing, which entered the boiling fat in enormously thick batter with no hot flat surface to meet them. Oh, the joy! The battered fish was OK too, but the savs were my favourite. On real takeaway night I'd try and eat them in a slightly offhand manner so as not to cast aspersions on Mum's valiant efforts.

If we kids were feeling flush we could call by the shop for a ha'penny's worth of scraps. These delicious morsels were, and still are, the free-floating batter crumbs that are scooped occasionally from the hot fat and dumped in a pile to the right of the vat. What a treat: a newspaper scoop of hot, crispy fat all to yourself. You had to walk the long way home to get rid of the evidence. Past the white dome in the middle of the intersection of Riverslea and Ellison roads and past the 'other' grocery shop, the one that never seemed to sell anything you actually needed. Just a lonely old man in a long grey smock coat behind the counter in a dim interior lined with giant biscuit tins.

Was it the poor people's shop, I used to wonder, in my unconscious imperious fashion. It was, though, where I picked up my *Dandy* and *Beano*. I have no idea why I split the source of my comic buying. Did I think it was somehow fairer to give all commerce in the neighbourhood a chance at my custom? Nothing about my methods and motivation at that age would surprise me.

The greatest drain on my, and everyone else's, resources was the Saturday morning trip to the Embassy cinema for our weekly threepenny fix of Hopalong Cassidy serials or an exhilarating hour or so of the *Cartoon Parade*. I loved these even though I could never convince my temporary brother, Ray, that the characters weren't actors dressed up.

I'd figured out exactly what they were: moving drawings. Even when I ran an extreme example past him, like the scene of Tom (of *Tom and Jerry*) running through a fly-screen door and then crumbling into a pile of cubes as a result, he would fall back on the old trick-photography argument.

But it was the cartoon parading that got me — the seemingly endless succession of titles. Was that the last one? Is this the last one? As the *Woody Woodpecker* credits rolled, the Walter Lantz logo with the little knight on horseback sporting the long lance ('Lantz', get it?) would appear. Is it all over? Or, wait for it, boom! The MGM lion would roar out of his cartouche and the *Mighty Mouse* banner would appear. God, the joy. By the time the actual end arrived you were sated, done, happy to totter down the long, tatty, carpeted lobby to the street.

Then we would wheel our bikes up the footpath to the Ernest Adams bakery, where you could buy these crude prototype ice blocks — homemade things that were just flavoured water in large trays with flat sticks poking up at all angles from every metal divider. The person at the counter would graunch the big metal handbrake back on itself and shake out the icy bricks. So icy that your tongue would stick to the frosty surface on the first lick — and stay stuck for a town block or two as you negotiated your bike with one hand and eased the ice block's hold on your tongue with the other. It became a competition to see how long the stupid thing would adhere.

But then real ice blocks came to town. Robinson's put on a bit of a field day. The item in the spotlight, the novelty that had the whole town in its thrall, was something called a TT2. What a peculiar label. Pure genius really — so mystifying, so exciting. Was there a TT1? Did we miss out on that one? TT, of course, stood for Tip Top. And the 2, oddly enough, stands for the next tier down from dairy, i.e. ice cream. I guess the proud owners, and creators, of the Tip Top brand didn't quite trust anything without ice cream in it.

Anyway, on the big day, Robinson's gave them away and we queued for miles — well, at least half a block. You could pick up your freebie, walk back up the road to the back of the queue and eat it as you inched your way forward, finishing in time to get a fresh one. No one I knew went back for a third one, so it didn't break the Robinson bank, and what joy it brought to the neighbourhood. We talked about it for months. Then the dam really burst: Topsy, Pink Topsy, Jelly Tip, Strawberry Toppa and a weird orange concoction called, if memory serves, a Jaffa Top. I think it bombed. The fantastically labelled Moggy Man didn't turn up until the 1960s, and I've got an original Frizzell Moggy Man poster in my 'archive' to prove it.

On my quest to expand my comic-buying budget — now we had, as well as *Superman*, Aquaman, The Flash, Green Arrow (and Speedy), *Batman* (and, yes, I know), Captain Marvel (and the whole damn family) and *Green Lantern* — it quickly became obvious that I was going to have to get an after-school job to complement the kindling chopping and the lawn mowing.

So I canvassed the neighbourhood and landed a job at the chemist shop. My job description was delivery boy and I even had a bike with a basket on the front to scoot round on. My task was to deliver prescriptions, 'scripts', to housebound pensioners and such. I'd pedal off to the address — all local, naturally — go up onto the verandah, knock on the door and wait for the footsteps up the hall, or the loud croak from the depths of whatever creepy old dump I found myself in. Sometimes I'd find myself in the kitchens of these gloomy houses, standing in a stifling fug of old people and wormy wood, proffering the box of pills or tub of ointment and wondering, with some alarm, how I could politely extricate myself. I didn't want tea in the tannin-stained cup or a mouldy biscuit, and I certainly didn't want to sit down and have a chat.

I kind of got used to it until I hit my delivery nadir: a cranky old coot who lived in a house in our street that we had always assumed was abandoned. Wonky gate, collapsed letterbox, totally overgrown with untrimmed trees and all manner of creeper — the only bits of house visible, like gutters and architraves, falling away from their fixings. And here's young Richard bushwacking his way from the front gate, up the rotting steps to the verandah and knocking timidly on the front screen door — or what was left of it.

After the usual interval of deathly quiet I could hear the now familiar grunting, huffing and shuffling from the gloaming, but this time it sounded like the skeleton army from Jason and the Argonauts coming up the hall. What was all that rattling?

I was seriously tempted just to deposit the package on what was left of the step and Indiana Jones it back through the liana vines, when the door opened. Mr McGregor came right out and stood on the verandah, towering over me and waving a big cigar box half full of pill bottles. Stiff grey hair bristled from every pore. And this was what rendered me mute and virtually paralysed: he was wearing grubby pink long-johns with trousers and braces and the top half of the blotchy underwear had obviously been close to his heart for a very long time, because great white corkscrews of chest hair were growing right through the woollen weave of the roseate vest.

He gave me that 'What are you staring at, you stupid boy?' look, grabbed the package from my nerveless grasp, shoved the cigar box into the vacant claw, then turned with a great waft of mothballs and strode off back into the darkness of his cave.

I stood there pondering my future as a chemist shop delivery boy, but the money was too good. And I liked being out back of the shop in that little room with the viewing window. As well as counting out pills, using a nifty little flat plastic shovel thing with a trough/funnel arrangement on one side into which you tipped the counted pills before funnelling them directly into the bottle, I was also tasked with mixing and casting peculiar little jelly bullets called pessaries.

I'd mix up the gloop, pour it into a rubber mould like an ice-tray with regimented rows of inverted cones, swipe the excess off with a deft scrape of a spatula and put it aside to set. I'd then fold the mould inside out, pop out the jelly bullets and put them in an Agee jar. For what, I didn't know, but I did notice that a lot of women bought them. Even when some information did seep through, the idea of an intimately placed, frothing bullet never really made a lot of sense.

I overheard a lot of weird and personal stuff as I lurked out the back, more than a 12-year-old boy needed to, and in the end I wasn't sorry to say goodbye to the job. All those stammering young men working up the nerve to ask for Durex, and loud and bolshie matrons discussing their rashes. It was a relief when the year ended and Dad got me a stinky job in the Dickensian bowels of the freezing works.

Not a lot of need for Robinson's dairy at this point either. Coca-Cola had come to town and we would gather up at the Excel Dairy in town to spend our Bible class collection money and sit in 'booths' beneath large posters of bright young American bobby-soxers waving the oddly shaped, glistening brown bottle in the air, moisture artfully beading round the famous logo. (When I first read in my American comics of Archie Andrews or Dagwood Bumstead drinking a mysterious beverage called Coke, I had imagined a glass of water with actual lumps of coke clonking around in it. Surely not?)

My *Knockout* days were petering out too, and I was getting my *Phantoms* and my Carter Brown novels from Foster's bookshop two blocks down from the Excel. And I had plenty of young sisters to go and buy the frozen peas for Mum.

Aunty Clarrie beaming in.

19

THE NAKED PIE CART

Bob and Clarrie Arnold, Uncle Bob and Aunty Clarrie. My instinct tells me that Clarrie was Mum's friend: the way they could laugh each other to tears would tell me that, whereas the vibe around Bob was always a bit askew. He was quite an intimidating fellow. Tall, like Clarrie, raw-boned, unruly red-blond hair and relentlessly cheerful. He looked a bit like a popular comic book cowboy character of the time called Red Ryder (look him up — it'll help the story) but instead of Red's Little Beaver sidekick, Bob had Clarrie. Same haircut, different height, gender and race, and also relentlessly cheerful.

The two of them were like a couple of hillbillies who'd struck it rich and were convinced that the pay-off was only a day away. Bob drove a huge 1929 DeSoto Model K with solid wheel rims where the wooden spokes used to be. This beast was already an anachronism when Bob bought it. Flash wheels like those on Ford's Zephyr Zodiac were already turning up on the streets of Hastings.

It was never quite clear just what Bob did for a living. He and Clarrie would disappear for months at a time, then magically appear in the driveway, grinning like they'd just robbed a bank. Bonnie and Clyde they were, same initials, without the tommy guns. Just the Eliot Ness car.

They got married somewhere along the line, and the reception was held at home. Bob was dressed like a mobster: high-waisted pants, voluminous white shirt buttoned at the wrists and a wide American tie. Hair still out of control. Clarrie had a veil somewhere between a fascinator and the full deal, scissored off at shoulder length and perched up on her thick auburn hair. She wore it all day, bopping about, waving her angular Ozarkian elbows in the air.

I remember the food: Mum went all out for her old friend. Trestle tables set up in the hallways were loaded with great heaped plates of corn and cake. A bowl of boiled-up frozen peas, all mountained up in the middle, threatened to avalanche down and over the lip of the bowl. I'd never seen so many peas in one place, at one time. Frozen peas were a once-a-week treat in our house. They came in a frozen slab about the size of a Dick Francis novel and which Mum would lower gently into a saucepan, where the peas would slowly disengage from the mother-ship until the pan was roiling and boiling with bright green bullets. The pile of sausage rolls was also a daunting prospect.

What next for Bob and Clarrie? Waimārama, it would seem. They'd found a primitive shack in the scruffy poplar woods down by the river and rented it for the duration. This collapsing pile of fibrolite could hardly have been a romantic idea. Whatever the plan was, it was decided that young Richard was going to be a small part of it. So I climbed into the back of the DeSoto and off we roared over the rolling hills of Hawke's Bay to a beach community that felt 100 miles away from Hastings.

Why was I always scooped up for these mad escapades? This could be complete vanity, but I think it might have been my odd Forrest Gump demeanour, and my drawing. It seemed to confer some sort of otherness on me, made me special to have around. Or perhaps easy, like a dog. I'm only thinking about this now, 70 odd years later, but it does account for many of the situations I would find myself in. Like bunking down in a possum-infested whare in the middle of the Waimārama bayou.

The noise on the tin roof at night was terrific — the scrabbling, screeching and ch-ch-ch-chattering. A lot of it seemed to be actually *in* the roof, just above the Pinex, and the suspicious-looking yellow stains coming through the warped panels tended to confirm this. I lay there, staring at the ceiling, with the musty eiderdown pulled up over my mouth.

In the morning, after my Kornies, I went out onto the front porch and there, standing on the paspalum 'lawn' looking at me, was a girl dressed in a light blue frock with a white waistband and a white, rounded collar. She looked like the young blonde girl who waves to Marcello Mastroianni across the estuary at the end of *La Dolce Vita*. She looked like a mirage.

Turning on her heel, she gestured for me to follow, and off I went: into the tangle of silver poplars, blundering along behind this strange girl, who skipped and hopped through the tangle of rotting and listing trunks as if she was negotiating an open meadow. We kept this up, along the riverbank, through the silver light — a Jack Russell pursuing a firefly — until we got to the sea, from where we walked back along the road to the house.

I don't remember saying much, except that I learnt she was called Margot, a name new to me. I fell instantly in love, then never saw her again. Was it something I never said? Maybe she just went back to town. Whatever it was, I know I'll never forget her. Clarrie seemed to know something about my mysterious 'girlfriend', teased me a bit in her laughing way. She bought me a jigsaw puzzle — Captain Marvel (the Shazam one) busting into the lab of the evil Doctor Sivana — which took my mind off Margot, and the possums.

I never did find out what Bob and Clarrie were doing down there in the woods but it didn't work out and they did their disappearing act again, until a year or so later when they popped up running a pie cart on Ōhope Beach, just over the hill from Whakatāne, and I was recruited once more. Mum put me on the Newmans bus with a wind jacket and a small pasteboard suitcase and waved me off. She must have really trusted Clarrie, and Newmans.

We had to change buses at Rotorua, though no one told me about that. I wandered aimlessly around town with my little brown suitcase, and found a miniature golf course, complete with windmills and volcanoes, where I played a round or two. Mum must've put money in my pocket. Somehow, miraculously, Forrest Gump got back on the right bus and made it to Whakatāne.

This time Bob and Clarrie had graduated to more salubrious accommodation, a proper house two blocks back from the beach. I had to share a bedroom with a rather dishevelled individual who reeked of Silver Fern tobacco and a weird sort of man-only funk. I'm not sure whose cousin/brother/in-law he was but he kept to himself on the other side of the room with his race books and beer.

What a summer that was. Even a hideously swollen toe from a shell cut didn't spoil it. Clarrie drove me, in the DeSoto, to a doctor in Whakatāne who said he was going to lance it, which put the wind up me a bit because I immediately pictured the lances from my King Arthur books. But whatever he used, the results were dramatic: the toe emptied out like, well, a lanced boil. I hobbled off down the main street with Clarrie, who bought me a spiral-bound sketchbook and a little tin box of those irritating watercolour cakes that bleed into one another all the time. We went home and the invalid painted, from a calendar in the kitchen, a picture of three yellow, floppy-eared puppies sitting in a sewing basket. It was pretty much all I could see from my perch at the kitchen table. A couple of plasters and a swim in the sea saw me back on duty at the pie cart in a day or two.

I suspect Bob kitted it out himself — bought an old plywood caravan, sawed a hole in the side, covered all the cuts with half-round dowel, put it up on blocks, took off the wheels and Bob's your uncle. Basic, basic, basic. Not a scrap of decoration or signage on it — the very opposite of the bright and breezy hotdog caravans at the Easter Show in Auckland. Same on the inside: counter, cupboards and cooktop as straightforward as a woodcutter's cottage. Everything white, even the food: peeled potatoes, batter, parboiled sausages, pale sticks, paper napkins. Thank God for the big dunking bowl of tomato sauce.

I had two jobs. One was to drop the peeled potatoes one at a time onto a steel grid, then push them through it with a long lever like a homebrew bottle capper. Voilà, chips. My other responsibility was inserting the pale sticks up the sausages' backsides so Clarrie could dip them in the batter and fry them up on demand. I loved being in there, above the customers, Clarrie chattering away as she bustled about in the small space, stocking up the pie warmer, Bob coming and going with his tools.

His greatest achievement was a long-drop toilet he built in the mānuka up on the slope behind the pie cart so we didn't have to keep running back to the house all the time. It was half hidden in the bush but still partially visible from the road and the beach. You didn't have to shut the door; I'm not even sure it had one. The most creative aspect about it was the actual toilet. Bob must have used the one out of the caravan because it consisted of a toilet seat attached to a kind of drum arrangement that sat above the hole. The point I'm making is that it wasn't connected to the actual construction of the shed it was housed in.

Sitting on Bob's throne one day, I leant on the downside of the shed to give myself more purchase as I ripped a piece of newspaper off the wire hook and the whole thing started to tip. I hunched my head down between my knees and made myself as small as possible as the entire structure arced over my back with a great screeching and creaking, and crashed several yards down the hill. The toilet paper went with it.

I sat there dazed and amazed, looking out at all the people on the beach and the customers coming and going to the pie cart below me. I crab-walked down, retrieved the toilet paper and sorted myself out. Clarrie never heard it go, wouldn't believe me when I turned up at the caravan's back door (the original front door) breathless with excitement after my brush with public exposure.

Oh, how they laughed at drinks that night round the kitchen table. More drunk than usual. I crawled off to bed early but the party went on into the night, Clarrie's mad cackle echoing down the hall. Eventually the noise died down and my roommate came bursting into the bedroom, reeking more combustibly than usual, and began prancing round the dimly lit room like a circus pony, moving closer and closer to my bed as he did so. Then he came to a lurching halt at the head of my bed, pulled his horrible great sponge blob of a penis out of his tweeds and waggled it in my face, all the while growling, 'Eh? Eh? Eh?'

I backed myself up against the wall and just glared at him/it. Then Uncle Bob appeared, silhouetted against the hall light, arm out-thrust to hold the door back like the cover image of a cheap detective novel. Bob's wrath was terrible to behold; I thought he was going to kill this wretched individual, who I'm thinking probably wasn't a relative.

Summer was over. Time for Richard to take his plastered toe, his art materials and the beat-up valise and get back on the bus. I guess Mum and Dad eventually heard some version of events, because I never returned to Ōhope, although my brother Bill, 15 years my junior, tells me he went and worked for them in a fish and chip shop there. Bob and Clarrie had moved up in the world.

I've still got the watercolour of the puppies.

Pinocchio, the author's pet Romney lamb.

20

THAT BASTARD BOXTHORN HEDGE

Of all the chores delegated to me the one I dreaded the most was clipping the boxthorn hedge, a particularly evil stretch of flora that flanked the wild half of the property, the 'section'. When he bought 507, Dad had scored a double quarter-acre: two sections side by side. It was an odd partnership — the proud old villa surrounded by its ancient and rather grand landscaping, albeit on a slow slide back to wilderness, right next to an actual wilderness containing the continuation of the drive, the garage, bean fence, clothesline, walnut tree, vege garden, asparagus patch and Mum's putting green.

By some antique and colonial logic, the civilised planting along the northern street frontage — herbaceous borders, yellow oxalis, flowering shrubs and a large magnolia tree — gave way to this monstrous wall-of-death that ran the entire length of the section all the way down to the driveway exit. It must have been about 20 yards long, over 6 feet high and 5 feet deep. That's a lot of hedge. Even mowing around it was a hazard. Leftover clippings that had evaded the raking of my last effort lurked in the grass like thumb tacks.

But the trimming was a truly frightening prospect. No shorts and bare feet on this job. It was a pair of Dad's old white work overalls, a heavy jersey, gumboots and a massive pair of stiff leather mittens from the freezers at Tomoana, and a bloody stepladder that had to be dragged up, down and around the great green wall.

The sides were bad enough, except maybe that sweet spot at chest height where all hostilities were briefly suspended and the clippings fell straight to the ground instead of into the bib of your overalls and the tops of your gumboots, but the top was a total curse. Like giant bits of barbed wire, the clippings lay where they fell and you had to lean out, into the hedge, wearing those bloody great gloves that felt like they'd been modelled out of plywood, and flick, scumble and swipe the clippings out of the brambles and onto the ground. *And* I could only lean over so far, which meant leaning in from the other side on the home run. *And* you had to rake as you went or you'd be pushing the stepladder through accumulating piles of thorns. People used to toot in sympathy as they drove past, seeing this brave young man on a stepladder weeping silently as he took his puny clippers to the boxy behemoth.

No chore was too much of a chore after the boxthorn clip. We didn't call them chores back then, of course, though the term was starting to creep in from the American comics like *Archie* or *Blondie*. In Hastings we called them jobs, and mine were all miniature manly outside jobs, like chopping the kindling.

It was a once-a-week job, down by the woodshed. The lean-to kindling woodshed behind the garage, that is, not the great water-tank-on-its-side woodshed where all the big stuff for the living room fireplace came from. I rather enjoyed the task because it was down in one corner of my walnut tree kingdom — the big pine chopping-block stump firmly anchored in a small space between the woodshed and the huge blue-gum stump with its flax bush skirt, and the surrounding area covered in a deeply satisfying mulch of bark and chips, all hidden away from the house.

I used a big axe to further split the split wood into library-book-sized slabs, then I'd switch to a tomahawk (love that word) to reduce the slab to kindling. With a good, evenly grained slab you could, holding it vertical with one hand, go chop, chop, chop, chop, in from the outer edge with the tomahawk, and the kindling bits would spring off towards the gumtree stump with a clean and exciting plink, plink, plink.

The trick was to release the last bit standing just before the last blow fell. I didn't always get this right and still have the diagonal scars over the first knuckles of the first and second fingers on my left hand — diagonal because you're holding the slab with your hand, fingers extended downwards at 45 degrees, right?

After a robust session I'd gather all the pick-up sticks and dump them in the tea-chest in the corner of the washhouse until it was full. Once, perhaps in a hurry, I artfully stacked the tea-chest in a way that made it look full with only three-quarters of the usual volume. Dad, impressed by the speed with which I'd accomplished my work, stopped by for a look on his way to the toilet as I laid the last couple of sticks. He looked at me, paused, then reached down and gave the box a vigorous shake, causing the level to drop down to where it should have been. He looked at me again, grinned and said, 'I tried that trick myself when I was about your age.'

On occasion I would hang about down there playing with my Mohican tomahawk, whacking it deep into the softly furred surface of the chopping block. Somehow I discovered that if you hit the top of the corrugated iron fence between my corner and Mr Langford's garden cleanly enough, the tomahawk would make a very satisfying bite into the galvo. How do you stop doing that? I gradually chonked my way along from where the fence met the woodshed to where it ran into the gumtree stump. The top of the fence looked like an upside-down buckskin fringe. Very attractive in a Davy Crockett sort of way, though the long-suffering Mr Langford didn't seem to think so.

Filling the coal bucket was a once-a-day job. The coal shed was right by the back steps where all the men drank beer on a Sunday, in the base of what would've once been a tank stand. It had a rickety, white painted tongue and groove door kept shut with one of those short, windmilling latches.

Once a month or thereabouts, the coal man would deliver the coal. A cheerful fellow, naked to the waist, all sweaty and streaked with coal dust and wearing the most unusual garment: like a sacking jerkin, open down the front, with a sacking hood, he resembled a character out of King Arthur or Robin Hood. After parking his big flat-deck truck loaded up with sacks of coal out on the street, he would back himself up to the deck, reach back, grab a sack by the 'ears', pull it onto his sack-clad shoulders and then just lean forward and take off up the drive. It usually took him about six runs to top up the shed, and with a friendly wave — how white his teeth looked against his sooty face — he'd be gone.

I hated delivery day because it was hard getting any purchase on the pile with the metal coal shovel: you had to jiggle and fiddle to get a shovelful. The trick was to burrow down the side of the pile until you hit the concrete floor and then you could shove the shovel in under the coal with a lovely grating sound and get that damn bucket full in time to get back to your Superman comic.

My only inside job was cleaning out the flues of the coal range, which was actually quite a satisfying job — no crawling up the chimney. I had a small arsenal of tools for every flue and would lift all the little cast-iron hatches off their flanges and blindly scrape and sweep all the soot in relays from the topmost flue, where the chimney met the stove-top, to the catch-all tray at the base of the oven.

Because you couldn't see what was going on you had to do it by feel, and you *could* feel the soft, pillowy soot flopping down through the flues as you raked and shuffled with a special tool like a poker with a flat flange at the base sticking out at 90 degrees. And the big reward: how much soot did you get? Mum seemed to find it all quite fascinating as well, looking on in her apron as *Doctor Paul* droned on from the radio in the background. I'd rake out the pile of soot and rust flakes, wrap them in newspaper and take the bundle outside to the rubbish bin.

And then I was outside again, ready for the next challenge — the lawns, second only to the hedge in scope and significance.

You started the mower by wrapping a short length of cord around the flywheel and giving it a good heave, and another one . . . and another one. Once you got it going you sort of toggled the cord round the handlebar and it swung there until a low branch whipped the top of the spark plug off or one of Mum's pegs jammed up the blades, instantly stalling it.

Like everything else, except the hedge, this job was carried out with bare feet. One day I was mowing after a week of rain and the mower was making pretty heavy work of it — great clots of wet grass clogging up the blade bearings and bunching up along the horizontal rod that was meant to keep the back roller clean. In the reckless manner of the extremely frustrated, I reached out with my foot to wipe away the offending clumps, and watched in horror as my big toe disappeared underneath the rod and the tin housing above it. I quickly, very quickly, reversed the machine, and got my toe back, minus the nail. Not good. It got me out of mowing the rest of the estate — got me out of a lot of things — and had me hobbling for a few weeks until the nail grew back.

I remember the day I noticed the new nail creeping up out of the mangled quick. I was staying at Aunty Nora's place in Pukerua Bay, where she was teaching at a one-room school. We'd been for a swim at the little beach below her house and the time in the seawater had stripped the wounded toe of all loose material. There it was, a brand-new nail. Funny thing, memory, isn't it? The sandy track down to the beach, all the pine tree roots sticking straight out of the eroded banks and me sitting on the sand staring at my toe, thinking my invalid days were over and I was about to be valid again, about to be back behind the mower.

The lawns around the house were a tortuous circuit — so many trees, shrubs and borders that you were nearly always going in circles. Dodging under the strawberry tree limbs (good for sitting in, eating the small fruits), hopping around the monkey puzzle tree hoping for a prickle-free run, swerving around the built-up bed of the big palm, trying not to dislodge the fancy brick edging which, despite my best efforts, got less fancy over time. No one seemed to notice.

Mum and Dad had inherited this mini botanic garden but had a wonderfully superficial appreciation of it. I know that on a Sunday, especially if I'd done the big mow on the Saturday, Mum liked to get out in her best frock and take Dad by the arm for 'a tour of the estate'. (I vaguely understood that the words were said with a hint of irony.) And it did look quite stately, if you overlooked Dad's take-no-prisoners pruning techniques, the gaps in the herbaceous borders and my muddy mowing skid-marks round the skeleton of the camellia tree (one of Dad's more impressive prunes). The layout must've had great bones because it was obviously taking a lot to ruin it.

My favourite bit to mow was Mum's putting green because you could go straight up and down, and even, on a good day, get two-toned green stripes. This, though, was very rare, given Hawke's Bay's vicious summers, and also because Dad's burning pile, where all clippings went to die, was right in the middle of it. Mum gamely ignored the big scorched spot in the middle of her mini golf course as she lined up her first shot down the range to the Wattie's baked bean tin sunk into the scrabbly turf. Once you managed to get the ball into the tin, you could do it all again in reverse, back to the tin at the other end. If you overshot on the first hole you lost your ball in the unruly ferny tangle of the asparagus bed.

The more or less rectilinear nature of the golf course released me from constant manoeuvring and I would stride out and sing. With the din of the Morrison shattering the peace and quiet I presumed that no one could hear me as I bellowed the lyrics of, say, 'Splish Splash' at the top of my voice. Yes, Bobby Darin in the area. Years later several friends told me that they could hear every discordant note as they walked past on the other side of the hedge of death.

On Sunday evenings the fire was lit in the ornate Victorian fireplace in the living room and we'd all gather to play Chinese checkers, do jigsaws or play that card game with the big octagonal board . . . what was that called again? On this particular evening we were all gainfully employed in front of the fire when we heard Jack Porter and Dad clattering about in the kitchen. The screen door slammed, and the two of them appeared in the living room door like Livingstone and Stanley. The great white hunters returning from a rabbit shoot up at Kereru Station.

Dad stepped forward, knelt down, unzipped his cotton-duck windcheater, and a lamb hopped out. Lost . . . no mother . . . they couldn't leave it behind. It was gorgeous. Perfect little face, tight grey-white crinkly wool, tiny hooves. It skittered and slithered around on the polished wooden floor that skirted the Persian carpet. I scooped it up and that was it — I had a pet lamb. We got some milk into it somehow and shut it in the washhouse just outside my bedroom window and I lay there all night listening to its plaintive bleat.

The next day Dad came to light with a 44-gallon drum and some straw and we set up a possie for the lamb in the corner of the golf course, where the big hedge met the magnolia. The big drum was laid on its side and the inside was generously scattered with straw. The lamb took to it immediately. I called it Pinocchio — my current hero. He was, though, in fact a she, a Romney, and she turned out to be a relatively low-maintenance pet. She had to be tethered all the time, obviously, but she never seemed to mind — just sat over there in her corner looking like a lamb under a magnolia tree. I took her for walks, took her to school, took her home again. Took her to pet day at the A&P show. Got a ribbon. We all got ribbons.

She loved eating the magnolia flowers. If you fed them to her by hand she would delicately nibble the waxy petals, leaving an arc of little teeth marks in the pinky white flesh. Otherwise it was milk, for weeks, from a big bottle with a black teat, always a frantic operation with the milk foaming and coagulating at the corners of her mouth as she bunted and sucked, her tail going crazy like a separate animal. She always went down on her front knees, as lambs do in the paddocks, which was handy as you didn't have to raise the bottle above waist height. And did she grow. Every time I got home from school she seemed to have got bigger.

It must have been near the end of her bottle-fed period, six months maybe, that she got a bit too much for me to handle: the shit shovelling, the straw changing — and the lead tangling. What a shemozzle that was. She'd go around from the front of her barrel and into the back (why was it open at both ends?) and then back around again and again until she couldn't move. I'd have to shove and heave her round in the opposite direction to get her free. Yes, I know I could've unclipped the lead, but how do you wrangle a sheep with one hand and detangle six yards of lead with the other?

After a few weeks of this Dad suggested that it might be time to 'take her back to the farm' — obviously a euphemism for a one-way trip down to Tomoana. I don't know if I twigged to the true story but I was well over it by then. Having a pet sheep hadn't been part of the plan.

So off she went. I think we dined off her for a couple of weeks. How long does it take for a large family to eat a sheep? It's only four roasts and a couple of lamb racks, isn't it? I *sort* of knew I was eating Pinocchio, but not convincingly enough to run weeping from the table. Anyway, meat on the plate is such a different order of reality from a bright-eyed ball of wool nibbling a magnolia flower, isn't it?

So, no more Pinocchio, but I couldn't mow that corner of the section without thinking of her — not until all the pugged-up mud dried out and the grass grew back. And by then the time had come to cut the hedge again.

The ubiquitous pea.

21

CANNERY ROW

They weren't actually in a row and there were only two of them and they were, in fact, about 3 miles apart — and only one of them canned anything. But what a Steinbeckian continuity they represented: the women mingling in the quad at smoko with their hairnets and smocks, the men playing euchre in the canteen.

The big one, the one that was so big it was pretty much a row all on its own, was Wattie's, and the smaller one, the one that only froze stuff, was called Fropax, probably because they froze things in packets. It's taken me years to figure that one out. If you couldn't get a job at one of these great labour sinks, you could always get a job at the other. And if you were so totally incompetent that you couldn't get a job at either — and to be fair, they did employ more women than men — you could always find employment at the freezing works. And, wonder of wonders, there were two of them as well: Tomoana and Whakatu. My loyalties were obviously with Tomoana because Dad had a bit of pull there. In fact he got me my first job at the works when I was about 15.

I was in the lowest of the low, down in the dank and wet pelts department. Anything less like a department you couldn't imagine: a dark and dingy satanic mill, all low stud and grimy windows keeping in the constant stench of rendering tallow and whatever the hell they treated those pelts with.

I loved it. The best job — the most responsible job — involved dragging on a pair of enormous rubber gloves and scooping pickled sheepskins out from these grotesque wooden vats of God knows what acidic muck and flinging them behind you with a matador cape flourish that flicked them out like a throw-rug onto a pancaked pallet stack. If you couldn't master this complicated manoeuvre by lunchtime they moved you onto one of the really vile jobs, such as stirring and pugging the slimy hides into the horrible thrall of the great horizontal rotating wooden paddles that filled up half the tub. That prospect alone was enough to encourage some serious flourish practising. No smoko till Barcelona.

From those salubrious beginnings I worked my way up, season by season, to the small goods department where all the 'nice' people, like school prefects and university students, sorted out the tangled piles of guts and offal as they tumbled down from the floor above them. In fact, the entire process from killing to tallow was gravity fed. That's why the confused and highly suspicious livestock had to be driven up these long and precipitous races from the holding pens way down on ground level. Often they'd be led on their way by a 'Judas' sheep. Only the sheep, I should say; the cattle were just herded . . . like cattle.

The killing floor. The loudest, most dangerous, biggest dick-swinging community in the works all worked on the top floor. And the slaughtermen were the top of the top. Large, loud, confident men spinning their knives like drum majorettes, shouting loudly to no one in particular as they sliced through briefly exposed throats before another gun-slinging twirl saw the knife back in its scabbard. Some showmen kept the blood-soaked blade held out to one side like a cinema villain while others did the draw-kill-reholster thing every time.

These implacable showmen, standing at their raised platforms like Inca priests, revelled in their exalted status, and the loudest of all were two bat-shit crazy brothers named Slats and Darcy. Slats because of his improbably long Sam Hunt legs, and Darcy because that's what his name was, and it seemed the perfect fit for a short, wiry maniac.

Slats seemed to lead the numbers game from his lofty perch, sending the still-kicking sheep down his slide at an astonishing rate, while Darcy roamed his separate kingdom over in the cattle-beast corner. In full production this meat machine was pure bedlam. The cattle bellowed and stomped, the killing hammer exploded regularly with the force of a .303 rifle. The chutes clattered and crashed as the huge beasts collapsed to their knees. And all the while Darcy swaggered about like a demented ringleader, reeling off a running commentary about nothing that I could ever distinguish. It was hard to tell just what he was actually meant to be doing, but one of his most obvious and dramatic responsibilities was the bloodletting — gathering the fresh blood in a bucket for the black pudding.

When the dead beast was hauled aloft by a hind leg and attached to the overhead chain mechanism that propelled it along to the various dressing stations, Darcy would move in underneath the enormous dangling head and jab his butcher's knife straight up into the jugular vein. The bright red blood would instantly gush forth, and this was Darcy's big moment. Up would come the bucket to catch the torrent while he stood there like a rock, feet planted, head to one side, yodelling and hollering while the blood poured and splashed into the bucket — and all over Darcy. When the flow finally exhausted itself he would do a triumphant circuit of the floor with blood-clotted hair, grin beaming through the gore, knife aloft and swagger on full throttle. 'Shut the fuck up, Darcy!' his brother would shout from his vantage point over by the mutton chain. More ritualised banter. More blood for the pudding.

On one spectacular occasion a cattle beast somehow managed to escape the confines of the chute, scrabbling in terror out and over the top of the high rails. As if the regular atmosphere of hissing steam and bellowing animals wasn't bad enough, we now had an enraged steer loose on the floor. Everyone instantly dived for cover, except Darcy. He holstered his knife, took off after the deranged beast and caught it by the tail. At first it looked like he was just along for the ride, skidding and skating over the wet concrete, sparks flying off his hobnail boots, until it became apparent that he was somehow in charge. By twisting and turning the cow's tail he managed to steer the beast — steer the steer — until he had it cornered long enough for the hammer-man to pull his dreadful trigger.

Another one of his many and various tasks was blowtorching stray tufts of hair off the sides of beef after the skinners had ripped the heavy hides from the swaying carcasses. His favourite prank was to sneak up and play the flames onto the seat of a fellow worker's trousers as they swapped rude jokes with a colleague. Given the heavy twill the men favoured, it would take a minute for the heat to seep through, giving Darcy time to be far enough away to watch as the recipient of the prank leapt into the air and angrily turned on the prankster, who was on the other side of the floor cackling like a fool.

Being so low in the pecking order, I thought I was immune to all this blokish tomfoolery and was surprised to find myself a recipient of the hot seat treatment. For some odd reason, in my case, the heat took so long coming through that Darcy came back for another blast — just as it hit me. I spun round to catch him crouching there, curious about my apparently insulated underpants, his blowtorch blowing onto the floor.

I suspect my obvious interest in his killing floor charisma endeared me to him in a weird way. He even came up with a nickname for me, Moses, because of my insipient, try-hard bohemian beard. This would have been 1958 or 1959 and, believe it or not, I would've been the only person on that floor with a beard. Probably the only one in the entire freezing works, apart maybe from a couple of poets on the small-goods floor below.

Where I should've been probably. Even though I was always relegated to the 'tidy' jobs on the chain — ticketing, tallying, shunting and so on — one day I managed to magic myself up to trimming, another of the more lowly tasks except that this one involved a knife, a scabbard and a steel dangling from your belt. Oh the glory, my own knife. The job, trimming odd bits of skin, wool and sinew off the carcasses that the big boys further up the chain had missed, was a bit of a doddle really, except that I kept trimming myself; I've still got the scars. Too many shaky Mondays after long weekends in Napier. Eventually they took the knife off me and moved me way down the line to the cooling floor, where the dressed lambs were shunted into graded rows before being bagged and hauled off to the freezers.

Oh, the freezers. My father's ammoniac domain. What a goldmine that turned out to be when I finally got into it. The shift started at 2 a.m. and continued with breaks until 10 a.m. The work wasn't so much hard as weird. The passageways and the chillers themselves were so iced up it was like stumbling through endless ice caves, all of us shuffling along like molemen in the dim light, hardly speaking because of the cold. The main job was to unhook the rigid mutton — gloves within gloves, immobile leather mittens — remove the steel gimbal and push it off down iced-up wooden chutes to the waiting railway wagons outside. That's all you did, over and over again, emerging every hour for fresh air and half a fag.

After six hours of this numbing routine we were transferred to the cooling floor, where we stripped off down to our singlets and inched our way along the lines of relatively warm meat with a huge stack of mutton bags over our shoulder, peeling them off one at a time and slipping them up the fresh carcasses, like slipping a pillowslip onto a pillow, and then tying it in a neat knot at the top. Over and over till 1 p.m. when they sent you home. Or, in our case, straight around to Wattie's to labour on the pea belt until quitting time. Big days, big money. Punching the clock just like in the movies.

Wattie's was fun, whether it was the pea belt or the tomato crusher, because you were always surrounded by women — fabulous, funny working girls, who seemed to laugh and chatter all day, playing netball in the breaks and teasing us students — school and university. A few teachers would turn up for a bit of overtime as well, which always amazed me as we assumed they were all set up with 'proper' jobs. One, the music master from Hastings Boys', would fall asleep with his elbows on the pea belt, which would drag him off his stool and onto the floor, whereupon he'd clamber back into position and do it all again. To be fair, it *was* a mesmerising process: staring at a moving sea of peas, picking out twigs and frogs' legs. When the belt stopped for smoko the rest of the factory appeared to get up and move in the opposite direction. Very discombobulating.

I managed to manoeuvre myself into a sort of non-job where I walked around with a shovel and a bucket scooping errant tomatoes off the concrete and tossing them back into the vats. And that's how I met Trixie.

The air in the cannery was constantly sexually charged. All those bright and carefree ladies (they weren't really called anything else back then) larking about and teasing the men. The men responded in kind, of course, the increasingly risqué banter rising above the constant din of the cans clattering overhead and roar of the steam vats. Maybe it was the noise that encouraged the banter, the notion that you might be only half heard . . .

Trixie and I ended up working together on a contraption called a palletiser, a relatively new packaging invention designed to speed up the loading of another logistical marvel called a pallet (which came with another nifty novelty called a forklift — exciting times).

The trick with the palletiser was to keep on top of the rows of cans delivered by rails from overhead, and to know when to spread the cardboard spacer over the finished layer just in time to start a new one. Trixie and I got pretty good at it; it kept us busy and it kept us close. She more or less claimed me as her official palletiser sidekick, which soon meant that wherever I sat for smoko, Trixie would be right there, chatting with her mates, me vaguely attached to the edge of the group. I was secretly quite flattered. She was obviously a lot older than me — possibly, looking back, about 40 — but she had my full attention: dyed blonde hair up in a jaunty ponytail, lots of ribbons and colourful neck scarves, ballet flats on her tiny feet. She looked like a character out of an *Archie* comic.

Then she asked me out on a date, said she'd come by 507 after dark and pick me up in her sporty little turquoise Triumph Herald. What had seemed like a vague schoolboy fantasy back at the cannery was getting way too real. Waiting, I was so nervous that I could hardly breathe. And suddenly, there she was, sitting at the wheel of a little perfumed car that looked as though a full wastepaper basket had been emptied into it. I'd never seen so much make-up on a person. Was that rouge?

Trixie got cracking the minute I shut the door — arms, elbows, knees, bucket seats, brake, gear stick and steering wheel, rear-vision mirror and sun visors. It was a bloody small car. And I was a complete shit. I broke away, made up some lame story, threw open the passenger door and bolted, hiding in the house panting like a greyhound until the wee car slowly drove off. I never returned to Wattie's.

A 1936 Austin Sherborne.

22

THE AUSTIN TEN-FOUR SHERBORNE

Who'd cover a car with pikelets? Butter side in? I had a pretty good idea. It was exactly what that Havelock North bus gang would do.

I'd got close enough to this curious crew with my school lunchtime shenanigans to be invited to an end-of-year party in one of the rich people's houses that dotted the slopes behind the village. I think it belonged to the owner of a flash menswear shop in town, and I don't think the party was his idea.

I got dressed up in my best (and only) grey slacks, borrowed the Austin and drove up the hill and up a long, looping-in-and-out drive lined with conical conifers. I kept on driving right around to the exit gate, where I parked by a big hedge, out of the way. I was a bit self-conscious about the picture the funny old car painted.

The house looked huge, a three-storeyed, pebble-dash Tudorish thing with multiple mullioned windows and a row of gables sticking out of the tiled roof on the third floor, and all lit by outside lights in the garden and by the pool. Lots of young people were milling about by the lights by the pool. I nearly retreated and drove home again, but I braved it, sidled in and found my Havelock mates, who suddenly didn't seem quite so matey. Friendly enough, but with the teasing ratcheted up a notch or two, like their noses. Odd. I'd never been anywhere where I'd felt this weirdly obfuscating cloud of privilege.

Gavin, the large fellow who'd sat on my head, greeted me warmly and showed me where the drinks and food were: a few pikelets and lamingtons, and lots of beer. What did the girls drink back then? The ubiquitous Pimm's? Wine hadn't been invented, port was a bit serious and spirits were what the grown-ups drank. Punch, I seem to remember punch. I do know I was taking it easy, with the Austin waiting for me down by the hedge.

Despite Gavin's efforts, I still hung back, mooching around as usual, Ishmael keeping out on the edge of the glow from the campfire. Mysterious rituals were followed. The boys got loud and the girls started jumping in the pool, fully dressed, their frocks spreading out like hibiscus blossoms. For a minute I pictured knickers and naked legs kicking about freely in the clear water under the umbrella of the floating frocks, and nearly stayed. The boys, arms around one another's shoulders, laughed and hooted like young stock and station agents, their ties askew and their carefully combed hair coming unstuck and falling forward over their foreheads.

If I'd known about drinking to cope I might have got into it but

I decided I'd had enough and quietly made my way back down to the car, which revealed itself with a strange mottled texture as I approached it in the shadow of the conifers. That's when I realised why there was a dearth of pikelets at the party: they were all stuck to the Austin. At least they didn't get to see my reaction. I took some pleasure in that. Only some. I vented as I peeled off the baked goods and threw them one by one into the hedge, then drove home in a car covered in butter.

I can't remember how I got rid of it. Mum would've wondered what I was up to if she'd seen me washing the car with hot soapy water at daybreak. Actually, I have a memory of wiping it down with an old rag in the big garage when I got home, smearing the butter around till it disappeared like cabbage on a plate.

How do you choose a car? How does anyone choose a car? Sometimes the car chooses you. Dad had had the Austin — strange, humble little vehicle — thrust upon him. Did he resent it? Probably, but he never grumbled about it and he serviced it dutifully and regularly, lying out there on his back in his white Tomoana overalls, fiddling about with drip-trays and grease nipples. He even painted it, the same colours as the house — green and cream. Same colours as his (soon to be my) bicycle. Same paint.

We drove out to Ocean Beach one Sunday, and for once, because he was usually meticulous about never letting the petrol level get too low, 'because of all the muck at the bottom of the tank', he had let the level drop to a point where, when he went to drive back up the long, very narrow, very steep gravel road leading from the beach, the petrol couldn't or wouldn't flow up the length of the car to the engine.

He had to turn the car round and back up. I can't remember if I was excited or terrified, but Mum kept yelling, 'Dick! Dick! Dick! Dick!' all the way up, as if it would somehow keep him on course. Mum was freaking us all out more than the actual event. The four of us in the back seat hunkered down so Dad had a clear view out the back window, which meant we could see his face throughout. Such a study in furious concentration and exasperation I've never seen since.

The glory days came when Dad was able to afford a new car. Well, maybe not a new one, but his one. He came up with this great lump of a thing called a Vanguard, a Standard Vanguard. It looked like the Hunchback of Notre-Dame going into a ruck. A cross between an estate car and a saloon, it was a sort of slate, bluey grey colour. How he loved that dumb beast. He immediately took us for a drive up the long, straight roads out the back of the Tukituki river. Got the speed up to about 90 miles an hour, every rivet and window mechanism rattling, the engine screaming fit to bust, Dad grinning like a maniac and Mum yelling, 'Dick! Dick! Dick!'

The arrival of the Vanguard freed up the Austin, for Mum, who had to learn to drive all over again, and for me, fortunately just turned 15. And so I learnt to drive as well. Hastings was so flat we had to do the handbrake start on the short, gentle slope that went up the railway embankment. Even then it took Mum about four goes to get it right.

Oh, the freedom of the Austin. Off down to the Tukituki on Saturday nights, hooning about in the gravel pits — kind of slow wheelies. I toppled the car once, but the gang managed to right it. No visible damage, apart from the dirt. Riverbed grit in the residue of pikelet butter. I even got a girlfriend at some point and bravely drove out to the river after a movie for a park-up, but ran over a possum on the way. End of that cunning plan. It's the thump and the bump that does it, isn't it?

I'd use any slender excuse to jump in the car. 'Need a loaf of bread, Mum?' Off I'd go, the long way — eight blocks up to the railway crossing, loop across to Heretaunga Street and back down around to the dairy. One day I was only a few blocks from the edge of the CBD, a remarkably well-defined thing back in 1959, when a kid on a bicycle wobbled into the intersection just as I was accelerating out of it. Next thing I saw him fly vertically up from the left front mudguard, legs and arms cartwheeling in the air.

Shit! I pulled over, got out, went back and there was my victim lying motionless in the gutter. I remember crouching down and saying to him, 'Don't die, don't die.' A circle of bystanders gathered in about a minute, running out from the Tulip bakery and Hutchinson's furniture store. A policeman seemed to instantly materialise, along with the mayor, a short Greek-looking fellow who also owned a 'prestigious' men's outfitters in town.

As the dazed boy shook his head and sat up in the gutter, I heard the mayor say to the policeman, 'He's OK, he's Dick Frizzell's boy.' The mayor knew Dad? And did he mean I was OK, or the boy in the gutter was OK? Whatever he meant, something must have worked. Nothing happened. Were there witnesses? Did the boy run into me, or did I run into him? No one seemed to care. The crowd dispersed, the policeman wandered back to the town hall chatting to the mayor, the boy limped off wheeling his mangled bike, and I drove home in a totally undamaged Austin, without the bread.

At the end of my last year at Hastings Boys' I had to borrow the car to ferry a ridiculous painting I'd been labouring over at home for weeks into school for the end of year presentation. And I do mean labouring. For some insane reason I'd chosen to base the picture on the tramping trips I'd been making out into the nearby mountains with a tramping club that I'd joined in my (or should I say Mum's) never-ending quest to find something that I might enjoy doing besides sitting in my bedroom drawing comics all day.

The scene was set on the verandah of one of the tramping huts we used to target as our destination — one boy moving towards another boy who was sitting in the doorway taking off his boots. What was I thinking? I had no idea what composition meant. The kid next door posed for both boys, which lent the narrative a peculiar stereoscopic air; the only point of difference I could muster was different-coloured shirts. And as I got down to details I realised that I couldn't remember whether the hut was made of wood or tin, what the door looked like, if there was a window? Did I have to put in a verandah post? How would you know if it was in front, or behind?

No one told me about reference: I just thought you were meant to know these things. But I battled on until I had two remote and totally disconnected boy trampers acting out a mysterious ritual against a vaguely wooden-looking wall with a rectangular hole in it. It was finished; the board was covered in paint.

So off to school I drove with my masterpiece in the back seat. Easy enough, and good fun driving into the school grounds, parking under the trees where all the teachers parked. Everyone thought the painting was amazing, never having seen a painting in their lives. One wonders what they were actually seeing.

Come lunchtime and my friends decided that it'd be a great idea if we all went for a bit of a drive. Well, how was a chap going to say no to that simple request? All five of us piled into the boxy Ten-Four, me and big Gav in the front and Simon, Leo and Noel folded into the back seat like the Three Stooges on a two-person settee. I remember looking in the rear-view mirror and thinking, 'If Simon farts in here it's going to be horrendous', and already that sly, wide smile was starting to spread over his mug.

But where to drive to? Well, there's always only one answer to that question in Hastings: up Te Mata Peak. So away we went, the four old cylinders thumping away as I ground my way up and down the gears, double declutching like a pro, staring at the temperature gauge, willing it to behave. And we made it, parked and got out to let the car cool down. Looked over the edge at all the kitchen appliances on the slopes below, thrown over by people simply to watch them smash. Looked at the curve of the bay all the way up to Māhia Peninsula. Seen it all before. Then we climbed back into the car and took off cautiously downhill.

Somewhere near the bottom, as the road went from gravel to tarseal, the car suddenly dropped on the rear right corner with a dramatic graunch and stopped dead while we all sat there agog, watching the wheel of an Austin Ten-Four Sherborne go bounding off down the slope ahead of us towards Hastings.

Leo loped off down the road and retrieved the wheel. Gavin got out the jack and cranked the brake drum up out of the impressive hole it had cut into the asphalt. It was a bit hard to figure out just what had happened because half the wheel-nuts were still there on their bolts. It looked as though the wheel had been put on recently with an economy of security, and of bolts, meaning the wheel had enough play to eventually split the metal flanges round them, causing the holes to widen enough to finally let the hub pull right away from the bolts and the nuts.

Fortunately the spare was in passable form and so we put that on, with four nuts instead of six, and drove carefully back to school. After what was left of the shambles that is always the last day of school, I drove, carefully again, around to Dad's garage, the one he always used, and explained the situation.

I also nervously asked the owner if he could do the job without telling Dad. How did I ever think that that could happen? Who was going to pay him, for a start? Of course he told Dad. I was taken aside for 'a bit of a chat', which usually meant the dog collar coming down off its hook, but Dad didn't seem to be unduly fussed. Had *he* bolted that wheel back on with too few nuts? Hard to believe. Was it the fact that I was now quite a physically grown-up 17-year-old? Was this a manly thing, me misbehaving with a car? I had to contribute some of my Wattie's earnings to the repairs, basically a whole new wheel, and that was it.

I know that the Havelock North bus gang was impressed. They referred to it all summer — the wheel continuing on without us.

THE HASTINGS MUSICAL COMEDY COMPANY Inc.

Officers 1961

Patron:
W. E. BATE, Esq.

President:
H. L. SPENCE, Esq.

Vice-President:
W. WILSON, Esq.

Committee:

Miss R. HOWARD
Mr. T. BROWN
Mr. D. WHITWORTH
Mr. B. PETRIE
Mr. L. HODGSON

Miss B. STIRLING
Mr. P. BROWN
Mr. C. SPENCE
Mr. D. RICHARDSON
Mr. G. MITCHELL

Hon. Secretary:
N. J. TOOMEY, Esq.

Hon. Solicitor:
F. H. CORBIN, Esq.

Hon. Secretary:
S. C. TAYLOR, Esq.

Hon. Solicitor:
C. E. H. PLEDGER, Esq.

PRODUCTION PERSONNEL

Producer	LAURIE SWINDELL
Musical Director	ARTHUR YOUNG
Chorus Mistress	MARY BELL
Official Pianist	MARIE STOTHART
Costumes Designed by	RUTH PORTEOUS
Costumes Made by	RUTH PORTEOUS, RITA HOWARD, EUNICE SPENCE, FRANCIS MURRAY, Mrs. T. BROWN and Members of the Company
Scenery and Sets Designed by	HECTOR SPENCE and KEITH BRAZIER
Scenery and Sets Constructed by	HECTOR SPENCE
Scenery and Sets Painted by	KEITH BRAZIER
Properties	BARBARA STIRLING, PHIL BROWN TOM BROWN, LEN HODGSON and ANDY ANDREWS
Wardrobe	RITA HOWARD
Make-up	LESTER BULL, DIANE WHITWORTH, RAE LILEY, MAVIS STAYT, ROSALIE GEOR, MAISIE CHRISTESON, HILDA BLASONI, LESLIE HARRIS, JESSIE SWANSON and GRACE HUNT
Stage Director	HECTOR SPENCE
Chief Electrician	JOHN HENDERSON
Publicity and Programme	W. WILSON and T. BROWN
Business Manager	W. WILSON
Assistant Business Manager	D. WHITWORTH
House Manager	JACK HANNON
Prompt	GLADYS WILLIAMSON
Call Boy	RICHARD FRIZZELL

The Hastings Musical Comedy Company flyer for the 1961 production of *Officers*.

23

YOUNGER THAN SPRINGTIME

Did I get the job because I could draw? Did I get it because I was a personable young chap? Did I audition? I have no idea. But got it I did. In 1961 I became the call boy for the Hastings Musical Comedy Company's lavish production of *South Pacific*, the phenomenally successful Broadway hit. This was the biggest thing to happen to me since my appendix operation at the Hastings city hospital five years earlier.

I hadn't displayed any obvious affinity for the theatre before this, unless somebody with influence was remembering my outstanding performance in a Hastings Intermediate School production of *The 'Ole in the Road*, a vaudeville perennial about a toff on his way home from the opera encountering a gruff old roadworker night-watching a hole in the road. I wasn't the toff.

The nightwatchman seemed to have no idea what was in the hole but, at the urging of the toff, he went down into the hole with a match to have a look. After the explosion (managed how, I have no idea) I emerged with my face hurriedly blackened, to say 'Gas'. I remembered my lines; threw myself into the accent — 'Yes, guv', 'No, guv' — and thoroughly enjoyed the laughter and the applause.

On the strength of this brush with acting fame I sought out a small repertory company over by Frimley Park and signed up for the next production. This involved a lot of people talking loudly in plummy accents as they plunged in and out of either wing and a pair of french doors at the rear of the stage. All I had to do was rush onstage from the left with a pullover draped across my shoulders, wave a tennis racket in the air and call out, 'Gosh, where's Daddy?', then disappear out the french doors. But I couldn't do it. I managed it at rehearsal, but on the night I became so overwhelmed with stage fright that another cast member had to ad lib and accompany me through it.

But being a call boy was an entirely different sort of engagement; I never had to get nearer the stage than the wings. My number one responsibility was to run around backstage with an annotated script in hand and knock on the appropriate dressing room doors, thereby alerting the actors within to their impending entrances. Not that these eager amateurs needed any urging. 'Yes, Richard!' they'd call as I stood there in the corridor with my clipboard like a minor league soccer coach.

My oh my, what a glamorous job. I was right there in the thick of it — the chatter, the excitement, the nerves, the costumes and the greasepaint. I moved through it all like a ghost, practically invisible, just doing my job. But, and this is a big but, for a giddy moment, every night, I was front and centre. While everyone was getting into their costumes and putting their faces on, my other job was to paint the sailing ship on the stomach of the actor playing Luther Billis. Ray Walston had sported the original tattoo in the big screen production of 1958, and I had to reproduce this image of a fully masted brig, in greasepaint, on Bruce Logan's midriff every night behind the curtain. No pressure. Of course, I loved it, and it made me pretty much indispensable to proceedings. Wherever the production went, I went with it. We did a week in Napier, and as if that wasn't exotic enough, the show travelled up to Wairoa for a night. This was it: we were going to tour the world. The travelling circus had found me . . .

By this time I'd become utterly infatuated with Diane Kilworth, who was playing Liat, the exotic young daughter of Bloody Mary.

Bloody Mary herself was played by a famously loud and confident Hawke's Bay thespian called Sadie Brown. If you wanted an Irish fishwife or a Tonkinese street vendor, Sadie was your gal. She was incredibly kind to me, actually noticed I was there and gave me all sorts of advice about how to cope with the tender sensibilities of the leading actors.

Diane Kilworth lived several blocks down from us in a very modern, treacly-brown brick semi-detached with a cedar-shingled mansard roof. She'd go cycling past our place on her way down to the tennis courts at the edge of Windsor Park, long legs rotating, sandshoes on the pedals, pullover around her shoulders, auburn hair fanning out behind her as she breezed through the intersection. She must've been a few years out of school — probably about 19 or 20. I was obviously impressed, but I never thought much of it until I saw her lying in Lieutenant Cable's arms, with the backdrop moon shining over the island of Bali Ha'i, as he sang about Liat being younger than springtime . . .

Things move fast in musicals. I recently read the synopsis for the first time — all that time running around backstage meant I never actually listened to what was going on between songs — and what was going on was absolutely bonkers. Nellie the nurse from Nebraska falls for the oleaginous charms of the plantation owner, Emile de Becque, but backs off when she discovers that he has two 'mixed blood' children from a 'dark Polynesian' mother. Over in the American base, Luther Billis (complete with stomach tattoo) suggests a trip out to the forbidden island of Bali Ha'i to witness a 'ceremony of the boar's tooth'. Bloody Mary sings an ominous song about the island (my favourite song in the show) and Lieutenant Cable spends a night with Liat in a 'native hut', with Bloody Mary's blessing. Are you following?

Nellie washes a man out of her hair. American warships intercept and destroy Japanese warships, thanks to Lieutenant Cable's spy mission. Billis stows away on a plane and 'falls out over the ocean' when it's hit by anti-aircraft fire. Operation Alligator begins. Men go to battle. Nurse Nellie gets over her racial prejudice. Lieutenant Cable is killed, Emile de Becque isn't and sneaks in the french doors at the back of the stage to find Nellie bonding with the children and falls in love with her all over again. Some enchanted evening indeed.

Apparently Oscar Hammerstein adapted this mad story from James A. Michener's book *Tales of the South Pacific*, which he put together from diary entries, anecdotes and rumour he collected while stationed on a naval base in what is now called Vanuatu during the Second World War.

The performance in Wairoa was it, the end of the road, and the beginning of the long drive back. But I'll never forget the camaraderie, the sense of weary triumph and the sadness on the bus ride home after the finale. Diane sat up the back with me, or at least in the seat in front of me, possibly because we were the youngest in the team, possibly because she was impressed with my greasepaint skills or possibly because the seats up the front were all filled. Big stars first.

Everyone sang, of course, and not necessarily *South Pacific* songs, though Sadie could always be talked into 'Bali Ha'i'. Mostly they sang songs from other musicals: *Oklahoma!, West Side Story, The King and I, Annie Get Your Gun.* And a scattering of radio hits. Everybody trying to outdo each other.

It was like a very long repeat of the trips back from Napier, during which Diane's big turn was a fabulous rendering of the Johnny Mathis song 'Misty'. The ambient mood of the bus, roaring along through the pitch-black Hawke's Bay night, the interior softly lit like a bathysphere, everybody leaning out of their seats into the aisle as Diane trilled her way through the song, side-on in front of me, and I took it all far too literally. The bus dropped us off at the Municipal Theatre in Hastings and I rode home in the dark with my dynamo humming as I hummed 'Misty' along with it.

It was over: Dannevirke didn't want us, Levin stayed quiet. We all went home. My brig drawing days were over. Then Diane got in touch with me: she was going to have a party, a sort of cast reunion, at her place.

I worked hard in the intervening fortnight at imagining myself being 21 years old but naturally there was no way Mum was going to let me go to that little soirée. Being a call boy was one thing, but going off to a grown-up wine and cheese evening was another. She knew that pretentious semi down the road, with its mottled brown brick and sleek soffit. Too rich for Richard. It even had two front doors in the same gap — one a stained wooden slab with three vertical amber-coloured glass rectangles stepping down its face, and the second consisting of a fancy wrought-iron arrangement that looked like it was meant to cage the first one. Who did these people think they were? Well, this retired call boy was determined to find out.

When everyone was asleep or otherwise occupied, I dressed in the most urbane outfit I could muster — black jeans, white T-shirt and my crepe-soled brothel creeper desert boots — slid up my sash window, crept out over my drawing table and lowered it again, leaving a couple of pegs between the sill and the sash so I could get it open again. Then it was down the driveway, under the walnut tree, past the boxthorn hedge and off along Sylvan Road at a slightly hysterical jog. A block short I slowed down to steady my beating heart and then turned into the low-hedged crazy-paving path up to the uncaged front door. I pushed the buzzer and it was promptly answered by Diane, who invited me in with an ambiguous smiling frown.

The room seemed to be full of complete strangers. What had happened to all my comrades on the bus? On the night ride home from Wairoa, despite having removed their make-up and costumes, they still felt like the cast of *South Pacific*. But this lot looked like a tweedy echo of the crowd from that Frimley repertory theatre and Diane's tennis club. I spotted Bruce Logan, complete with off-the-shoulder pullover scarf and white shoes, who at least gave me a bit of an eyebrow waggle, and Sadie Brown came over and threw a meaty arm across my shoulders, though even then it took me a while to recognise her. I prowled around the edge of the nattering throng, thinking that maybe I should have worn something a bit softer, a bit more bohemian, something a bit less like James Dean in *Rebel Without a Cause.*

I kept prowling, taking in the coloured glass bottle things on the cocktail cabinet, Frank Sinatra on the stereogram, the Degas ballet dancers on the wall and the cheese and pineapple on the toothpicks. I sipped a desultory beer, chewed on a toothpick and sneaked out the door. No one noticed.

But this particular gift hadn't quite finished giving. A couple of weeks later, after I'd left and started at the freezing works, all the school was pulled back together for the end of year prize-giving. I shaved off my incipient beard, dug out my crumpled pile of navy blue flannel, and along with my fellow pupils reported for duty at the Municipal Theatre.

All of us were sitting in the stalls having a grand old catch-up as the teachers filed onto the stage for the run-through. The chattering and the shuffling subsided but then, '*Frizzell!*' I looked up and there was my old foe, vice-principal Chook Fowler, pointing sternly in my direction. '*Out back, please!*' God, not again. Not now, surely. But he meant it: one last go at turning Frizzell into a decent citizen.

I edged myself out of the row, walked down the aisle and up onto the stage (the same walk I'd make 24 hours later to receive my first for art and English) and off stage left.

I waited there for however long the run-through took to complete. Chook came out back, swishing dramatically in his black gown; gave me the usual phoney avuncular advice about trying a bit harder, all the while prodding my chest with his rolled-up programme notes. He then caned me convincingly, right on the spot where I used to stand and gaze out at Lieutenant Cable singing to a misty Liat lying in his arms.

It didn't hurt a bit.

The author with his youngest sister on Heather McInnes's horse.

24

AIN'T GONNA WORK ON MCINNES'S FARM NO MORE

I know that the name Frizzell comes from the Fraser clan, so maybe that had some part in how Dad linked up with a dour and irascible Scotsman called Jock McInnes, who managed Kereru Station, a huge farm up in the foothills of the Ruahines west of Hastings. This spread was so big that it was like a separate country — well, maybe not separate so much as all the country. You couldn't see it for country.

Between the picnics and the rabbit shooting we saw a lot of it. As Dad drove the Austin over primitive tracks out to the mighty Mohaka River to picnic on the gravel banks beneath huge pumice cliffs, I remember thinking, 'Are we still on the farm? Can you have such a vast geological thing on your own property?' Because our little gatherings were indeed dwarfed by these white formations, with the swimming hole beneath scoured out deep and blue by the mountain range upstream.

When I went rabbit shooting with Dad we explored a lot of country, ranging far and wide, over gully and knoll, dragging that bloody bag of beer bottles or rabbits all the way. I suspect it was the rabbit shooting that got Dad up there in the first place. We never hung out at the farmhouse and certainly never saw the McInnes family at our place in town. But one year I found myself up there working in the school term holidays.

Whose idea was it? Did I volunteer or did Mum and Dad think it'd be good for me? A special mission to toughen up that dreamy little bugger? With a fabulously beaten-up old trilby given to me by one of my 'uncles', I packed up my sugarbag, tucked my baggy daks into my socks and we were away. I was happy enough to go; I just didn't know what I was letting myself in for.

The house was up on a rise looking out at the mountains. It was an extended bungalow, with lots of add-ons and extras at the rear: mudroom, washhouse, woodshed, etc. The usual assortment of sheds, kennels and garages rolled out along the driveway that led up to a roughly defined turning area. I remember a horse looking over the fence by the clothesline with its fork-tipped mānuka centre pole.

There was a Mrs McInnes, and a daughter, Heather, about my age. The horse down by the clothesline was hers and she let me ride around the house paddock in the first few days of my stay. I can't remember Mrs McInnes saying a word to me after the initial greeting and Heather wasn't a great talker herself. McInnes himself might have had something to do with that. With his shaggy eyebrows and whiskery chin jutting out aggressively under a lipless mouth he was an intimidating sight. He obviously wasn't one to brook any denial. I never saw his hair: he always wore a huge tam o' shanter, big as a preserving pan lid, complete with pom-pom.

For the first couple of nights I bunked down in the spare room in the main house. But listening to McInnes play his awful Kenneth McKellar records, ridiculously loudly, was way too much: 'Roamin' in the Gloamin'' for breakfast. And the salt — I'd never seen anyone use salt like Jock did. He even poured — 'sprinkled' would be totally inadequate in this instance — it on his porridge. This seemed to me about the last thing you'd use, but at his insistent Scottish urging I gave it a go and was stunned to find it entirely appropriate.

Mind you, even the porridge itself was something else. I don't know what was in it but it certainly had a completely different texture to the rubbery frisbee of spinning-in-the-milk grimness that Mum served up. Coarse and friable, McInnes porridge fell from the saucepan like cowflop, maintaining a rough ziggurat of concentric circles that sucked up the full-cream milk like a volcano in reverse. And then you poured salt all over it. Creamoata was never going to be the same again.

After one of these hearty sessions of bagpipes and salt, McInnes took me down to the stables and gave me a horse, my ride for the duration — a huge, black, uninterested beast called Trigger. Standing next to him was like standing next to a truck. His back was as wide as a chesterfield. I had always imagined that sitting on a horse would be a bit like sitting on a motorbike. I hadn't anticipated such crotch-stretching width. Was Jock being slightly mischievous partnering me up with this monster? Probably.

He taught me how to saddle up. I couldn't possibly have thrown the saddle over the back of this great barn of a thing, but I distinctly remember the lecture about the cinch, how it had to go around forward of the full width of the belly and up into the 'armpits' of the front legs so it wouldn't work loose as you rode. He forgot to tell me that this bastard equine would puff his evil black stomach out as you tightened it so that the cinch felt more comfortable when he exhaled.

On my first outing, with Jock and everyone within a 100-mile radius watching, I set off at a lumbering trot down to the end of the house paddock. Just before we ran into the bottom fence Trigger turned, unbidden, and headed for home. As I jiggled and bounced in the saddle, the world before me began to cant alarmingly to one side as my badly cinched saddle slowly slipped sideways around Trigger's mighty flank until I was riding along like an Apache closing in on a defensive covered-wagon circle. I let go just before my point of view was completely inverted.

But I persisted with Trigger — I had no choice — and quickly learnt that if you slapped and punched his heaving ribs determinedly enough as you tugged on the straps you could stop the slippage. The only way I could get up into the saddle was to get him over to a fence and use the rails or the wires as a ladder. He farted a lot in merry syncopation as he trotted along: trot-fart, trot-fart, trot-fart. He very rarely responded to the gallop command, no matter how hard I heeled him in the ribs, but when you got within coo-ee of the barn he needed no second bidding and just took off, possibly even reaching something approaching a canter, and all I had to do was hang on.

Now that I was a 'farmhand', one of the first of my rural chores was to bundle up my stuff and move down to the workers' accommodation, known as the whares.

I left a relatively comfortable spare bedroom with an eiderdown and floral wallpaper for a creaky row of attached cribs that looked like a sad motel built by colonial settlers. They looked more like stables or kennels except for the four-panelled doors, the sash windows and the long verandah down the front. Only one of these shabby units looked lived in, which meant a rough pathway had been worn up the steps and over the verandah, through the cowpats, horse apples and windblown pine needles and dirt, to the door.

I followed the track with my swag over my shoulder, opened the door and there, sitting at the table rolling a cigarette, was the occupier, Eric. What a rough-looking bastard he was: unkempt red hair, freckles, goofy overbite, big bony shoulders — none of his grubby cuffs reached his wrists or ankles. 'G'day!' he said, as if I'd just popped out for five minutes and had returned with the milk.

One square room, two beds, one on either side. One table, two chairs, a chest of drawers and a short length of kitchen bench. A build-up of dust and dirt accumulated around the skirting boards. Eric's shitty boots sat at the end of what was obviously his bed — and the word 'bed' implies a false degree of civilisation.

I plonked my stuff onto my barely upholstered wire-wove and sat down at the table opposite Eric. What did we eat? Where did we wash? If this was a cowboy movie there would have been a horse trough out front where we washed our faces in a manly manner, but if there was one I must have blotted it from my memory.

I'll never forget Eric, though. Eric and his non-stop porn

commentaries, his sexual conquests: fanciful versions of such borrowed scenarios as the pool cleaner entertaining the lady of the house, in which he creatively made himself the star. So far in these stories I haven't used the word 'masturbation' once, but the time might have arrived where I have no choice but to deploy it. There is no euphemism I can conjure to describe Eric's dedication to the custom. Lying there in the dark on my mouldering cot, I'd listen to Eric work himself up with another of his nymphomaniac widow stories and then proceed to vigorously capitalise on the self-induced excitement.

As if working on a farm wasn't bewilderingly fecund enough. Everywhere you turned, some fearsome act of reproduction would be on display. Watching the bulls at work was an eye-popping experience. Why were their bright red penises so long? Couldn't they just get a bit closer? Maybe if the startled-looking cows would just stay put for a spell the bulls wouldn't need such extravagant apparatus?

All this was going on as I ambled past, sitting up high on Trigger, both of us out on one of my wool-plucking missions, life and death allegories at every turn. I'd roam around a likely ex-grazing paddock until I found a dead ewe, and my job was to get down and pluck the wool off the rotting carcass. This was a revolting and weirdly satisfying experience. If the bloated animal was at the right stage of decomposition the wool would just roll away like peeling the icing off a stale lamington. Sometimes the sheep would look as if it was still breathing, such was the great mass of maggots seething away inside it.

On any big station, the best fun can be the long days when people come from miles away to help with the big stuff, like shearing or docking. In this instance, dipping seemed to be in season, and what a mad and primitive ritual it was. Sheep, dust, dogs, men, women, me, all milling about in an insane racket of shouting, bleating, barking, whistling and sheep-race banging.

The freaked-out sheep were herded through the clattering, neck-jamming races to a short ditch full of evil-looking viscous muck where they slipped and stuttered down a short ramp until they were submerged up to their desperately extended necks. They then began to paddle frantically, eyes wide open and lips peeled back, down to the deep end, where some sadistic bastard, like me, had to plunge their heads under by pushing at the base of their necks with a long-handled tool that resembled a toothless rake.

This evil routine would ensure that the whole beast was dipped, but it also told you instantly which of these wretched animals was suffering with facial eczema. If the poor creatures were frantic with suspicion and dread before they went into the trench, by this time they were completely out of their minds and anyone down the business end of the trench got the blowback. This chaos went on all day, Eric spelling me on the plunging. We went to bed exhausted and reeking of sheep dip. Even Eric collapsed without his usual bedtime stories.

Sometimes Eric and I headed out together as a team. We'd trudge up to the implement shed, load up the tractor and trailer with posts, wire and staples and head for the hills. At some abstract triangulation known only to Eric we'd stop, unload and start fencing, obviously taking the lead from some existing point, though to me it seemed as if we'd decided to dig random holes in the middle of nowhere.

To say that Eric was lazy would have been to miss the point entirely. He just didn't seem to engage on any level, and when he did it was unhelpful. But things seemed to happen. We dug, pounded, stretched and nailed, and a fence of some sort would emerge from the tundra. And then McInnes turned up, took one look at our handiwork and went berserk. To this day I have no idea what we'd done, or hadn't done, but the frothing Scotsman grabbed one of the battens off the trailer and went at Eric like a Glasgow gangster. I just stood there in shock as Eric tripped, rolled and fended while the farmer whaled away until he was spent. It was a horrible thing to watch.

But when McInnes finally threw down the batten and stormed off, Eric got to his feet and rolled himself a cigarette, leaning against the trailer as if these mad dramas happened every day as regular as smoko. What a strange boy. I had begun to realise that he couldn't have been much older than me — just old enough to have left school and gone out into the workforce. Along with the dawning of this revelation came the parallel observation that Eric didn't like me very much. Did he think I was McInnes's pet? He certainly never saw him go at me with handy lengths of lumber and I suspect he had also figured out that I didn't really need to be working there and that this was only a soft sort of school holiday gig.

So he started to take out his rural revenge on me. All of a sudden I was the one stuffing up all the time. He went from passive to passive aggressive; nothing I could do was right. On one memorable occasion we were sent up a ladder with paint and brushes and instructions to paint the roof of the implement shed: a vast, flat, gently sloping plane of corrugated iron. Perhaps we should have started at different ends of the roof, but for some reason we began in tandem, moving back and forth in parallel lines. I have no idea what I did — maybe I was going at it too enthusiastically and forcing the pace a bit — but Eric got more and more irritated, needling me with snide comments and observations until he cracked and 'accidentally' painted right over my jandalled foot with an exaggerated swipe, then stood there with a sneer on his face.

To my absolute amazement, I dropped my brush and squared up to him. Now it was his turn to be dumbfounded. I stepped forward, and with one foot sliding about in its painted jandal, I wound up and unleashed a mighty roundhouse at his gormless head. And missed. I had another go with the other fist, and missed again. I was so wound up that I couldn't seem to get there. The muscles in my arms were locked in a mad akimbo rigor that inhibited any attempt at accuracy. But the general effect was dramatic. I must have looked madder than McInnes. Eric was certainly impressed. He even went off and found me a turpsy rag. He never said another word, just picked up his brush and got on with it.

We finished the job, and I finished up. School holidays were over. Dad came out and picked me up — from the house, not the whares — and drove me home. He quizzed me on the way down through the foothills, asked me about the silver paint between my toes. I didn't say much: told him about Trigger, and the salt. Never mentioned Eric.

The bridge at Windsor Park, Hastings, in the 1960s.
The bridge was constructed in 1934 out of rubble
from the 1931 Hawke's Bay earthquake.

25

THE GREAT PARK OF WINDSOR

I'm always intrigued by what leads certain public bodies to do good works. Perhaps I've been brought up on too many cheap Westerns, in which corrupt city councillors plot to rip off the hardworking and honest townsfolk, but it would seem that, despite the self-serving nature of the average citizen, a lot of astonishing altruism does take place. Even in seriously small and isolated communities someone always seems to take it upon themselves to make where they live better. It's just an extension, I suppose, of the rose bushes by the path leading down to the gate.

Windsor Park, Hastings. I usually steer away from research, on the grounds that I might find a truth that could compromise my carefully fabricated narrative, but in this case I've broken my rule and done a bit of homework. Way back in 1885, a certain Thomas

Tanner decided to carve 44 acres off his 1000-acre Riverslea Estate, bought from Māori, and create a park. When he was forced to sell up just a few years later, to an enterprising trio of gentlemen, the park was included. When, in the early 1890s, the local council couldn't afford to buy the park from this syndicate, one member, John Beatson, bought it and claimed naming rights. When Mr Beatson sold the park to the council in 1912, the details of the sale attracted the attention of the Audit Office and the transaction had to be okayed under a piece of legislation called, intriguingly enough, the Washing Up Act.

Then, in 1924, the Parkvale Golf Club was allowed to form a golf course and the Parkvale Progressive Society popped up to push for a swimming pool. A bit of slave labour is always handy: during the late 1920s and the Great Depression Mākirikiri creek was modestly dammed to create a boating lake and a tennis club was installed. Then came bridges, made possible by the 1931 earthquake, which, sadly, conveniently provided all the masonry material you could possibly need. Later there were paddling pools, park benches, lake edging, clever weirs and miles of steps and crazy paving. And in 1935, just when the park was looking its masonry and mortar best, the country celebrated King George V's Silver Jubilee and the good burghers of Hastings renamed the park Windsor.

From where we lived only a couple of blocks away, there were two entrances at our disposal: the dark side and the sunny side. We could walk or cycle around to the flowerbeds and lawns by the boating lake, or go down utterly treeless Sylvan Road to the much more mysterious tennis court entrance. The former welcomed you with great swathes of zinnias, the latter with an avenue of ratty black pines and a weird and ominous air of sexual frisson.

We'd formed a loose little group of secret smokers who gathered occasionally behind the tennis pavilion, just the lurking space for a spotty little gang of early teens to practise their boasting, bragging and bullshit.

Somehow, and definitely not on the club's agenda, our furtive huddle was invaded by an astonishingly bold and beautiful young Greek girl, who lived in a baronial-looking pebble-dash pile just up from Robinson's dairy. How she managed to infiltrate our outlaw non-tennis club I have no idea, but there she most definitely was, complete with a no-threat sidekick. Whoever she focused all her attention on thought they were it, but none of us ever was, even though it was insanely easy to convince yourself that you could be. It was really just a hyper-realised version of the usual boy–girl shuffling and mooching; she simply didn't know her own strength.

The atmosphere stays with me, though: the small, damp gap with the brick wall of the pavilion on one side, the clay bank towering over us on the other and our bikes in a tangled pile by the rubbish bins, the empty courts and the big, dark pines, and old Snoogles creaking by on his great black skeleton of a bike. All of this was only a short, uphill, curved pathway away from the welcoming zinnias on the next rise — darkness to light, tennis to boating.

What a welcome break from all that concrete the boatshed was, tidily constructed from slatted wooden uprights, painted classic Victorian boatshed green and nestled in nicely next to the low dam down at the southern end of the boating lake. The northern end of the lake was defined by a magnificent Art Deco bridge that stretched across the creek inflow like a brontosaurus with its tail on one bank and its neck and head stretched out onto the other.

One of the best holiday jobs ever (this was way before my Tomoana days) was helping in the boatshed. The way the sunlight filtered in through the slatting and the fact that half the shed went down into the water made it feel like a magic underwater cavern. I never tired of hauling the tin boats out of the storage racks ranged along the back of the shed and shoving them down the ramp, into the water and out onto the lake for the waiting customers. The other main component of the job was racing up and down the bank shouting out, 'Come in, number ten, your time is up!'

The canoes themselves were incredibly primitive vessels. It wouldn't be possible to design a more basic craft — green tin on a wooden frame and only vaguely canoe shaped, more like a stubby bayleaf, pointed at both ends with no obvious prow (no hydrodynamics whatsoever, except for the point), flat bottom, vertical sides and two flat triangular 'decks' fore and aft. The whole thing was about the depth of a beer crate. The only indication of for'ard was the boat's ID number brushed loosely on the prow in white paint.

We boatshed boys used the canoes too. What a mighty froth we beat up as we thrashed these ungainly craft through the swampy water. How much paramecium did we inhale in those ad hoc regattas? On slow customer days the more adventurous of us would punt under the low span of the brontosaurus and paddle further up the creek, where the landscaping along the banks quickly grew feral as you moved north, degenerating into a dense tangle of weeds, blackberry and willow.

At one point the creek bifurcated round an island, an exotic feature that became very much part of the upriver adventure. We'd pull our boats up onto the muddy bank and head off to explore the hinterland. All we ever found was the other side of the island, but it never stopped us hoping for a skeleton or a Māori palisade as we bushwacked where no man had gone before.

As the creek closed in again north of Treasure Island it became increasingly hard to negotiate, then virtually impassable, but what we did have up there were more creepy badlands, the gravel pits. These great piles, presumably huge dumps and mounds of leftover earthquake rubble, were big enough to get lost in and the whole site became our own private Arizona, where the goodies and baddies could fight from one dry gulch to another with fiendish weapons called shanghais, long strips of black bike-tube rubber with a slingshot pocket at one end. You held the leading end of the rubber in one hand and pulled the pocket, with a stone in it, back as far as you could.

Then you let the pocket go, at the same time jerking the hand holding the rubber forward and down — otherwise the first casualty of the launch would be your thumb. Although we went at each other with gusto, I can't recall anyone losing an eye. I guess all that hunkering down, like those Hopalong Cassidy gunfights, where we pot-shotted blind over the mounds of gravel, sorted that out.

In about the third year of our occupation the heaps were bulldozed away to make room for a skating rink. Perfect timing for me. I loved skating — the boots, the bearings, the wooden wheels, that little spanner thing.

Anyway, time to cruise back downriver, past all the eels and weeds, to the relative serenity of the boating lake. Just in time to pull another idiot up out of the weir. I would've thought it was obvious that a boat couldn't get down through the yard or so of cunningly stepped mini-dams that kept the lake full but allowed the creek to continue in its landscaped course to the camping ground. But there was always one.

I did it myself once. The actual dam was about as wide as the length of the boat but the slot where the water spilled over was the same width as the boat. The plan was never to shoot the mighty rapids — it was way too bluntly stepped for that — but the temptation was to just nose the front pointy end into that slot, join the gentle rush of water from the lake and just sit there, contemplating. But sometimes that flat bottom of the boat got a little carried away, literally, and then you just climbed out and manhandled the tin thing up and out again. Climbing down into it sans boat was fun, though, sitting cool and quiet with the water cascading down the mossy steps.

Up another curved path and onto the flats behind the boatshed was the playground: a very large concrete paddling pool enclosed at one end by an impressively long seat, like a stretched-out stone settee, where the mothers sat and chatted while their kids splashed and choked in the pool.

The design of it all was extremely elegant, considered and durable. It's still there. The swings, seesaws and so on were huge and definitely not for the faint-hearted. When you were standing up on the flat wooden seat of a swing the chains seemed to stretch upwards forever and, if you worked yourself up hard enough you could extend yourself out into space slightly higher than the pivot bar and hang there weightless with the chains going slack for a very long second before plummeting back on the return arc with a great knee-juddering jolt as they jerked back into action. It was exhilarating, that sense of extreme danger as you, chain and seat all seemed to part company for a second. It was a long way to fall.

The view from the swing's apogee, if you weren't in a death-defying mood, was over a vast expanse of flat grass that stretched all the way from the playground to the mysterious no-go zone of the camping grounds. It could've been a cricket oval, but it only had one function as far as I was concerned, and that was to hold the annual Hastings Highland Games. I suspect that the whole province got caught up in them, but the intensity was particularly noticeable locally. It seemed that anywhere you went in the town you could hear someone polishing their piping chops.

The games were always held on Easter weekend and seemed to go on all day, every day. And of course I could just walk over — no entry fee, no tickets, no fences, just a vaguely organised string of booths and stages ranging around the cricket oval. The faraway end of the attractions hosted a sort of mini version of those A&P show competitions. Many jars of very similar-looking marmalades going head to head with the bottled peaches, rows of flower arrangements whose winner always looked like an explosion in a compost heap — towering arrays of dead leaves, sticks and flower-like things erupting from exotic metal vases.

The vegetable judging was my favourite: lonely little displays of four beans or radishes in a row, accompanied by a certificate larger than the presentation. Imagine judging that, sucking seriously on your pencil, clipboard at the ready, eyeing the giant turnip further down the trestle with some trepidation.

These largely empty tents segued into the dance competition

stages, where things started to warm up. Earnest young women in what looked like full Scottish battle regalia leaping about over two crossed claymores or skipping and kicking around the stage in green shoulder capes with their arms clamped to their sides. And the pipers. Red-faced men with bulging cheeks and eyeballs, pummelling and elbowing their bags into submission, getting the pneumatics up to speed, practising walking and playing at the same time, out the back of the stage. And the outfits. Where do you store a thing like that? In a special wardrobe, with the mighty bearskin hat lying on its side on the top shelf? The pipes, boots and freshly whitened puttees arranged neatly below? The only rig I had to worry about were my skating boots out in the washhouse.

Another few stages along and things were definitely getting rowdier. The marching girls were beginning to make their appearance on the grounds. This was seriously serious stuff. These girls marched as if the future of their club depended upon it, and maybe it did. It was great to watch — the determined girls in their drum majorette outfits, short pleated skirts swinging over artificially tanned thighs, sturdy calves rammed into tightly laced-up boots.

The way they did that weaving in and out thing without bumping into each other always drew a great round of applause. As a spectacle, though, it tired quickly — I could never tell them apart — and so I would sneak off looking for empty fizzy drink bottles to cash in at Robinson's. I was always on the lookout for ways to keep those *Superman* comics rolling in. I'd reappear when the girls all went marching home.

Then there were the actual games.

Tossing the caber was always worth a watch: huge, fiercely

eyebrowed, bandy-legged men, wider than they were tall, staggering around the cricket oval in kilts and singlets with telephone poles cradled in their beefy hands down at sporran level and leaning back precariously against their mighty chests as they pedalled back and forth like juggling unicyclists, waiting for the magic moment to launch.

The object of this bizarre enterprise was to heave or toss the huge log high and far enough that it would describe a sufficient arc in the air to allow it to come down on its head with just enough momentum left to topple it further forward so that it came to rest with the cupped end facing directly away from the tosser.

The other great tossing event was the hammer, though I think it was actually called throwing the hammer. These men were a curious breed too, also huge and rather full of themselves, clapping their dusted hands together as they swaggered up to the mark. I don't know how professional these chaps were, but they were all remarkably erratic throwers: the hammer could fly off anywhere. Definitely not a sport to be watched from the sidelines; even a spot directly behind them didn't fully guarantee your safety.

My favourite was the wheatsheaf toss, a much more graceful and self-contained operation. It had its own little spot down on the bank of the creek, not far from our island. A spindly thing, like a narrow, etiolated rugby goalpost, was erected in the glade and the contestants had to use a pitchfork to toss, or flick, a hessian pillow full of wheat up and over the crossbar, which was raised higher and higher as the game wore on. The competition started early and went on at a gentlemanly pace all day, which suited me perfectly. I could keep going on a healthy diet of toffee apples and spun sugar and, because we lived so close, I could even duck back for another Easter egg if I felt peckish. I just had to keep an eye on the wheatsheaf heats so I didn't miss my guy.

These contestants didn't wear kilts but expressed their competitive seriousness in all manner of sartorial ways. My guy came on like a cross between an Australian shearer and a British coal-miner: high belted tweeds (complete with bowyangs), a sports coat over a white singlet, a short mutton-cloth neckerchief and an appropriately rakish brown trilby. He would amble up to the posts, take his jacket off, fold it neatly and place it at the foot of the nearest post, then carefully arrange his hat on top of the small pile. Interestingly, he wasn't a great barrel of muscle and haggis like the other tossers; he looked more like the 'ideal', sleeker, Mr Atlas illustrated on the back of my *Superman* comics.

He'd spit on his palms, rub them together, flex his shoulders and pick up his pitchfork. They all carried their own, like billiard cues. With weapon in hand he'd go over to the wheatsheafs and choose one. This was also a highly considered palaver that involved plinking and plunking individual sacks delicately with a single prong of the pitchfork until a suitable candidate was selected before it was carried, on one prong, over to the launch position. Then came the loading of the pitchfork, another matter of great precision. The pitchfork had to be inserted just so — not so deep that it impeded the launch, but not so shallow that it lost purchase too early in the build-up.

Having got it just right, and with the wheatsheaf dangling off the end of the prongs like an oyster off an oyster fork, he would flex his knees, rock his arms back and forth slowly, building up a strong but gentle momentum and, when the time was right, let fly. He won every time; I must have been to at least six games, and my bloke was always first. He never even bothered entering the early heats.

By the time the last sheaf had sailed over the crossbar and whumped back to earth, I was done. Sunburnt and spun-sugar queasy, I'd slope off past the tennis courts, past the pavilion of ill repute and make my way back up Sylvan Road, the last of the competitive pipers, or the lonely lamenting losers, wailing away in the background.

The author's mother not long
before the author turned up.

26

GJG

Gertrude Joan Gibson. Who was she? Yes, I know she was my mother, but who the hell was she?

I was her firstborn so she must have been youngish when she had me, but I have no memory of her being young. She was always middle-aged in my mind, with her blue rinse and her apron. Did everybody just leap into middle age at the end of the war? Men got their trilby hats and cigarettes, and women got their false teeth and queenly merino ram's-horn hairdos.

I know she looked girlish and stylish once because I've seen the photographs: slightly buck teeth, dimples and swept-up hair. I can imagine her at art school in Christchurch, painting her fruity fruit onto wooden bowls, hammering out silver ashtrays and forcing the initials 'GJG' into an interlocking monogram.

I've already written about how arty she was. Craft art, that is, not arty art. I don't know how the Canterbury College School of Art was structured back then but Mum obviously took the design option, which would account for her interest in craft. She left the actual art to the senior students, like Rita Angus and Olivia Spencer Bower.

She never uttered the word 'art', but she never lacked for an arty idea. That big house was jammed to the gunwales with her crafty hobbies, but Mum also loved fads. Whatever craze was sweeping the country, she had to be in on it: wire-knot puzzles, hula hoops, the fiendish red plastic pyramid and the Amazing Magic Robot — the angular viridian android striking a mashed potato dance pose as he spun round on a little circular mirror and 'always gave the right answer'.

Mum had a few little tricks of her own too. One of the most disturbing was the thing she could do with her eyeballs. If you asked, and she wasn't rushing hither and thither, she'd fix you with a freaky penetrating stare, concentrate like mad and her eyeballs would start to quiver, vibrating in her head like Lotto balls in their tumbler. Only for a moment, but it was a hell of a moment. For that brief spell Mum would disappear somewhere far, far away. I loved seeing her transformed like that, going into a world of her own.

The other world she would totally disappear into was that of the Singer sewing machine. She wasn't the only mum good at this, but with four daughters to fit out in frocks she was nose down in the corner of the kitchen/dining room a good deal of the time. Treadle, treadle, treadle . . . the belts and pulleys whirring away, bobbins rattling in the little compartment below the pulsing needle.

Clacking release lever and clicking scissors. Fabric ballooning out everywhere.

Even much later, when I was married and would breeze in on a trip down from Auckland, and she was curling up and shrinking with the cancer, her spine shortening like a game of Jenga as the bones degenerated, she would heave the machine up and out of its table and patch up the fraying cuffs on my denim jacket.

Mum was from quite a large family, the third in an interesting line-up of five. First off the rank was Uncle Jack, a big, ebullient bully who always seemed to be getting divorced and remarried. He built a very large boat on a rather small front lawn before going on to be the commodore of the Christchurch Yacht Club. So, a man of some substance, but also a superior being with his cravats and cufflinks. He mellowed a bit with age but was always patronisingly bemused by his younger arty sister.

Second in the count was Aunty Peggy Kelly — Margaret Nancy Kelly — well-known Wellington parliamentary reporter, journalist and biographer. And man, she looked the part: tweed skirts, plaid scarves, salt and pepper hair piled up, and chained-on spectacles for peering over, always on the go. She lived with her quiet husband, Bruce, down in the valley of one of those sloping Wellington suburbs, and had somehow ended up lumped with the job of looking after the family's matriarch, Granny Gibson, and her old duffer of a husband, Pop.

Gran was a very vertical old woman with a long cardigan draped from her dowager's hump and a duck walk like Popeye's girlfriend Olive Oyl. She was always preceded by a brown teapot clutched in both hands, either on the way out to empty it, or on the way in to fill it. Old Pop just seemed to drift about like a superannuated Billy Bunter with both hands looped in his watch and fob chain. He had Bill Nighy's condition, Dupuytrens contracture, where the last two fingers (usually) of both hands clamp down onto the palm. I was fascinated by this anomaly; he would let me lever the fingers up, then have them flick back onto the palm with a dull thwack.

Sometime before this odd anatomy lesson, my first memory — my first memory of anything — was of this avuncular English gentleman with his enormous white moustache taking me down to the Christchurch railway yards to see the puffing billies. I remember standing with him on the rear platform of a passenger wagon looking out at all the railway lines and the steam engines, a portly old man in a bowler hat and a very little boy having a moment.

Mum comes in here, but we can skip her because she's already been introduced and jump down to the twins: Hilda and Don. Hilda got the lion's share of the personality in that particular embryonic divvy up. I hardly remember Don at all, but Hilda was a mesmerising experience. To me she looked seriously exotic, like an Indian princess: large imperious nose, shadows round her fierce eyes and a massive head of dark, wavy hair. Quite terrifying to behold, but fantastically bawdy and good humoured, she married a butcher and smoked cigarettes.

Joan Gibson — she quickly dropped the Gertrude — second daughter of English immigrants. Where did all the art and design come from? Where might that talent have gone if she hadn't fallen for her spoilt young naval officer and devoted so much energy to breeding baby Frizzells? I doubt Mum spent any time dwelling on other scenarios — it wasn't in her nature — though she did seem to get a bit philosophical on that last stretch. I wish I could've been around more but my life was with my young family in Auckland.

I'd left Hastings, and Mum, in 1959 and gone off south to Christchurch, her home town. That's the whole reason I went there, to art school at Ilam instead of Elam, because Mum thought I'd be safer. Somehow her sister Hilda would keep 'an eye' on me. Funnily enough, I never saw Aunty Hilda the whole time I was there. And what the hell was wrong with Auckland anyway? Well, quite a bit, I suspect, in Mum's view.

That's where Richard Ernest Frizzell, the dirty swashbuckler, led her astray. My sister Valerie tells me that one of Dad's spinster sisters actually told her, after a few generous snorts of blackberry nip, that Mum had been a prostitute, some sort of Auckland ship girl, because otherwise how would she have stolen their golden boy away from them? (And, of course, anyone who hosted such large and unruly parties *had* to be morally corrupt on some level.)

Mum and her girlfriends were surely just attracted to where the action was, to the dashing young Merchant Navy officers in their white uniforms, brass buttons and epaulettes. Who wouldn't want to be there? On one of these merry cocktails-in-the-mess-with-Russian-cigarettes occasions, the boys took Mum and the gals down below decks to see their famous resident, the 'Wompo King of the New Zealand Merchant Navy'. This dishevelled wretch was laid out on his bunk, unconscious and unshaven after a boozy night out roistering at Ring Terrace. Mum and her friends marvelled at the state of the man, blew in his ears and balanced pennies on his eyelids, before retiring upstairs for more laughter and hijinks.

A week later Mum met her debonair blind date. And, yes, it was the king himself, all scrubbed up with his sleek smile and Humphrey Bogart cigarette poses. She was a goner, and lived 30 more years to regret it. Not in any burdensome, intrusive way, because they did seem to be fond of each other, but as a vague sort of existential background static, the echo from her own big bang, when Dad seduced her with the old, 'I may not come back from this, my last, Pacific convoy tour of duty.' I'm making this up, of course, but it would go a long way towards explaining Mum's weird attitude towards anything to do with sex and the great wave of modern social mores thundering down the pipe with the arrival of the baby-boomer generation.

Mum didn't like difficult. She insisted on happiness; unhappiness wasn't an option. If you made the unfortunate mistake of trying to tell her something true and personal about your life that she didn't want to hear, or believe, she would simply harrumph and say it wasn't so . . . and it wasn't. As we got older and started to move out into the world, we found that we had to lie to her constantly to keep her happy. Honesty had a hard row to hoe in our house. Maybe this wasn't unusual. More post-war trauma — dust yourself off, straighten up, keep on smiling.

And we liked to keep her smiling, even when she was chasing us around the kitchen with a wet dishcloth, we'd manage to turn the anger and frustration round as we leapt over the furniture like a mad monkey circus. Once we got that reluctant smile going we knew we had her and she'd plop down, red-faced, into a handy armchair with the cloth hanging limp in her hand and say, 'You wait until your father gets home.' But you could see she'd even forgotten what brought on the shenanigans in the first place.

So Mum kept herself busy. Constant motion was the trick, and there always seemed to be some sort of club that needed a hand with its entertainment programme. The kindergarten mothers' club ran regular little theatrical events at the local Presbyterian hall and Mum would be in like Flynn as unofficial director, organising skits and throwing the contents of her bottomless dress-up box at them.

I remember one of those nutty skits. Two rows of kindergarten mothers sit on the stage as if in a cinema, and a woman (Mum) comes in late and blunders along the row, stepping on everybody's toes as she goes. She pauses, embarrassed, and says, 'Pardon me, but I washed my feet this morning and I can't do a thing with them!'

Then she went mad on skiffle music, as if it was invented just for her. Our shonky little trio, the Brothers Mad, was doing a pretty respectable 'Rock Island Line', but Mum went all out, sewing up loud and brassy jazz shirts for all her kindergarten mothers and designing skiffle instruments for the carpentry workshop at the freezing works to whizz up.

Their biggest challenge was a long percussion instrument in which a row of assorted metal tools — a circular saw blade, a crowbar, a cowbell and several other metallic items whose function was more ornamental than musical — dangled from a galvanised pole suspended by two wooden stands at either end. Another item of great skiffle renown was an old broom covered almost entirely with loosely nailed-on beer-bottle caps — something else to assault the innocent song as you recklessly banged the floor with it.

But the star turn in this exotic line-up was the tea-chest bass. Dad was tasked with organising this, and in true engineering fashion he decided he could improve markedly on the original: a tea-chest, a broom handle and a length of string. Instead of the broom-handle being upright he fashioned a thing like a large guitar neck with the base screwed to the tea-chest and a big wooden machine head drilled through the upper end where you could, supposedly, 'tune' the string. It was almost impossible to play as you had to somehow crank the mighty key with one hand and pluck the string with the other, all the while struggling to keep the entire apparatus upright. But it looked great.

Mum played — oh, how she played — the beer-bottle kazoo. Again, Dad stepped up to the plate, dutifully emptying the bottles and cleanly removing their necks by tying two paraffin-soaked pieces of string around the shoulders of the bottles, setting them on fire and then plunging them into a tub full of cold water. Plink — two halves of a kazoo. One neck was inserted into another, with a layer of tissue paper between, and away you went, hum-singing with gusto through your beer-bottle trumpet. No lessons required.

Mum played everything with gusto: the piano, the kazoo, the percussion rack. Her theory seemed to be that if you played loudly and forcibly enough the din would somehow turn into music. And it sort of did, in a way. The two real musicians that Mum managed to coax into the line-up helped a bit.

My younger brother told me about Mum's command performance of 'My Old Man's a Dustman'. (Look it up, you young people. You don't know what you're missing.) The curtain opened on a lone rubbish bin sitting on the stage with the band leading off in the background. Right on the kazoo break, Mum jumped up out of the bin, dressed as a dustman, and proceeded to add to the cacophony. This was the same woman who had the nervous, throat-clearing cough and the bewildered fear of sex, drugs and modern art.

One little ritual she insisted on was the late-night check-in. No matter how rat-faced I might have been after a night's carousing, I had to creep up the hallway to the open door of Mum and Dad's bedroom, steady myself against the architrave, knock gently and quietly announce that I was home. I'd hear a gentle grunt and a snort coming from out of the darkness as she'd go, 'That you, Richard? Mmmm,' and I'd go crawling back down the hall to bed. I'd been a good boy once again.

All children lie to their parents, don't they? You'd be insane to expect them to share all their social secrets. But Mum seemed to almost expect us to understand and respect all her carefully constructed survival niceties. Dad, on the other hand, could see through the smokescreen. On the morning after one of my more spectacular hall-crawls, he took me aside and told me that he knew how wrecked I was and that he couldn't really care less, but if I slipped up and gave the game away to Mum he'd jump out of bed and plant me. There's a great double-hander for you: parental guidance counsellors.

But just in case you're building too negative a picture of this vexed woman, I want to describe a typical, and particularly memorable, Sunday roast midday dinner.

The Columbus radio up on its special little shelf playing the famous Sunday request session (Johnny Cash singing 'A Boy Named Sue'), Dad sitting like a laird at the head of the table, the leather strap on its hook by the servery hatch through to the living room. The five of us kids (the sixth, Bill, still to turn up or in a high chair) sat down the long sides of the table clutching our knives and forks in our fists like extras in a Charlie Chaplin movie. And all the while Mum running back and forth from the kitchen to the table, only pausing every now and again on the arm of a chair by the door between, apron balled up in her lap, always on call, watching for any lack.

On this occasion Mum came waltzing in, actually waltzing, to some familiar song, probably 'Tennessee Waltz', while holding aloft a huge roast lamb leg on an oval serving dish. Between the door and the table the entire leg slipped off the swaying platter and landed with a fatty splat on the lino. Without missing a beat, she speared it with the carving fork and managed to get both plate and roast to the table, while the song played on. It really was a magic moment: the sun shining through the large sash window behind me, Dad giving the carving knife a professional swipe or two and Alma Cogan now busting out 'In the Middle of the House' — and here it comes . . . right on time.

And for dessert: vanilla ice cream topped with Mum's homemade Kremelta chocolate sauce. This would set the moment it hit the ice cream and if you were cunning enough you could ease the melting ice cream out from beneath it until you were left with a sort of chocolate igloo sitting on your plate. *Crack*! Yum.

The whole palaver almost made the dreary morning at Sunday school worth the effort. What the hell was that about? Did Mum and Dad just want a bit of a sleep-in? Sex on Sunday? Even though

Mum was entirely incurious about religion, the idea of letting Dad 'bother' her on a religious holiday would've been a bridge too far. I suspect she was just hedging her bets by sending us off for a bit of Bible, so we would dutifully trot off to the aforementioned Presbyterian hall and sit attentively through the rituals.

I started to smell a rat when I was about eight. What was this Sunday school trying to teach me? I'd figured out that Monday, Tuesday, Wednesday, Thursday and Friday school was teaching me stuff that was somehow connected to getting on in the world, but what was the function of this weird and random add-on? But it seemed to make Mum happy so off we'd go. I'd take my short and silly tie off when I was two or three houses down the road (and tell Mum I took it off on the way home — more creative lying) and whistle along. I even rather enjoyed watching Mrs Davidson banging away at the piano, her bum poking out behind her on the piano seat and the pheasant feathers bobbing about madly on her black pillbox hat.

She was also a whizz at the felt-board, spelling out the Jesus story in front of us by slowly accumulating the narrative with little felt Marys and donkeys she'd pick out of a shoebox and magically affix to the green baize. (I was to use a similar narrative device in a series of paintings I did 25 years later. Nothing is wasted.) Ambling home knowing that the Sunday roast was ahead of us didn't seem like a bad trade-off.

Mum was a perpetual motion machine. Even with all the daughters and their designated chores, such as scouring the bath-tub, maintaining that huge old villa must've been like painting the harbour bridge. And that huge family to feed, clothe and shelter. Duty always called. I can't remember her ever sitting down at the table with us. I bet she even stayed on the move, rushing back and forth for the tomato sauce, on the Friday nights when we had takeaway fish and chips for dinner. She probably made the sauce.

Among my outside chores was taking out the compost. I remember taking out a mound of potato peelings in a square baking dish, coming back with the dish up my jersey and saying to Mum I wouldn't need any dinner because I'd just had a square meal. She loved that stuff: no joke was ever so lame that it wouldn't make her crack up. She would literally laugh till she cried. Even moderate calamities would set her off. As one of her cost-savers, she would put all her used Butterick dress patterns on a hook in the toilet and, yes, guess who got an overlooked pin in their arse one frosty morning. Mum seemed to think that that was a hell of a joke — me, not so much.

Years later, after I'd gone off to university, Mum and Dad planned an overseas trip and she went off and got a job for a bit of pocket money. In fact she got two: cooking breakfast at a local motel in the morning and picking asparagus in the afternoon. What a hell of a job. You stooped all the while, or you jogged along the rows on your bum, digging down into the loam with your knife to gather the fresh young spears. Mum was no fresh young spear herself at this time, but off she'd go, determined that she wouldn't be turning to her parsimonious engineer for spending money every five minutes.

The only thing that slowed Mum down in the end was cancer. They never did go on that trip. Slower and slower, and smaller and smaller, she got. Someone, probably her, had the bright idea of setting her bed up in the turret between the two verandahs — sun from all sides. She lay up there all day, like a princess.

I have no details of these days because we were living in Auckland but she still wrote her weekly letters to all her children. Six-page letters: five pages carboned and one page original. Just to be fair.

One day she put a boil-in-the-bag on the kitchen bench to thaw out for dinner before going down to the hospital for a routine check-up.

She never came back.

The author's Velocette
with its Navajo livery.

27

FIFTH IN LINE

Where did Ian Brigham get his money from? I never thought anything of it at the time, but whatever Ian dreamed up seemed to materialise. Want a sleep-out? A pile of lumber and demolition joinery would appear in his driveway. The driveway that Ian helped his stepfather lay.

Eric the Red, a little ginger cannon-ball who turned up and married Ian's widowed mother when Ian was about 10. Did Eric have money? It didn't look like it: they lived in a plain state house or state house lookalike up Riverslea Road — any place with a lonely, rectilinear and barren look was called that back then. Narrow hallways, featureless doorways, basic utilities . . .

None of this bothered Ian, of course, lying back in his sleep-out with his hand down the front of his pants, dreaming of an acoustic guitar. Which duly appeared. As did a large Ford Model T coupe, an antique even then, black as the rest of them and barely holding together; throttle on the steering column and spokes like a covered wagon. One day Ian turned up with it in the driveway at 507, honking that ridiculous ooga-ooga horn.

This car was basic. It couldn't have been more basic if you'd taken the engine out and walked it along like the Flintstones' fun car. It was so heavy and four-square on the road that it almost drove itself once you got it rolling. Coming back from an evening's drinking down by the river, Ian reckoned that he could steer by lining up the V created by the junction formed where the bug-eyed headlight stanchion met the curve of the left mudguard with the white line marking the edge of the asphalt. This often put the left half of the car into the ditch, which didn't seem to be a deterrent as it always somehow found its way back onto the rise.

The car's biggest failing was the radiator, which leaked like a sieve. We had to carry half a dozen flagons of water in the dickie seat wherever we went. Once, in a moment of breakfast-time brilliance, Ian poured a packet of dried oatmeal into it on the natural assumption that it would swell in the water and block all the holes. It seemed to work, until one spectacular night when the radiator blew — took the cap clean off — and the windscreen was instantly smothered with porridge. Ian calmly leant forward and turned on the wipers, but to very little effect.

Finding a replacement radiator proved to be beyond even his magic powers of manifestation and the noble Ford was retired, unregistered, unwarranted and, sadly, unwanted.

Undaunted, unruffled and un-anything, Ian went quiet for a couple of weeks before reappearing in our driveway with a large 1930s Plymouth sedan. Painted a creamy sand colour, it resembled a German staff car: long and low with a rococoesque radiator that leant back in a superior manner above a chrome bumper that curled out underneath it like a carnival barker's moustache.

This was an impressive beast. For some reason, possibly because he hadn't got rid of the Model T yet and Eric wasn't having it, Ian asked if he could keep the Plymouth at our place. The most unobtrusive spot I could find for something that seemed as big as a harvester when you got up close to it was down under the walnut tree in the lee of Mum's bean fence. She complained that every time she bent down to pick the beans at the base of the prolific vine she'd bump her behind on the monstrous mudguards and go headfirst into the foliage.

We took it for a run up to Lake Taupō once. Carried jerrycans of petrol in the boot and heated our cans of beans on primitive brick-built fireplaces at the side of the road. Ian wanted to pitch our pup tent (why were they called that?) right on the edge of the lake, which seemed like an adventurous idea. We erected the tent using dried raupō stalks as poles and settled down for the night, listening to the gentle slapping of the water on the pumice beach at our feet. The tide came in at sunrise — who knew lakes had tides? — simultaneously wetting the ends of our sleeping bags and softening the bases of our fragile tent poles. I don't know what woke us first, the tent collapsing or the water creeping up our bedding.

I don't know what happened to the Plymouth; Ian must have sold it because he suddenly turned up on a Zündapp, a 1954 Victoria (Vicky) III Zündapp, a sinewy olive-grey step-through with peculiar swept-back, extravagantly pinstriped cowlings and tear-shaped chain guards hunkered down over all moving parts. This odd vehicle, which looked like a Buck Rogers ray gun, also had the clunky streamlining of a German military vehicle. Where did he find such a thing? How did it even find its way to New Zealand?

Ian drove it around Hastings, sitting bolt upright in the saddle. It was a very impressive thing to be seen on while the rest of us were grinding about on clunky old Raleighs, with a three-speed Sturmey-Archer hub if you were lucky. Which I definitely wasn't, having inherited Dad's old clunker, which he'd painted with leftover paint from the house. Green and cream. It was like the Massey Ferguson of bikes.

I was cycling home from a mate's place at dusk, head in the clouds, playing a game I'd invented — pretending to be a regular, normal human for the benefit of any aliens observing us from outer space — when the bottom section of the front, cream, mudguard caught the erratic tread of the tyre and buckled up inside out, stopping the bike in its tracks and causing it to rise up vertically on the one wheel as I kept moving forward. Thank goodness the asphalt broke my fall . . . and the skin on my palms and knees. Let's see Brigham do *that* on his zippy Zündapp, I thought.

My post-Plymouth choice of wheels was a much more conservative purchase: a 175cc Velocette motorcycle, with a two-stroke Villiers engine — a detail that always had to be threaded into the description for some deeply technical reason. I stripped it down, which sounds way more professional than it actually was, painted it an odd sort of pale sky blue and covered the forks, guards and petrol tank with Navajo glyphs and symbols in black silhouette. Why, I have no idea. I guess I just fancied these flat schematic eagles and suns. The eagle motif looked particularly snappy on both sides of the petrol tank as I rode it to high school with my school bag balanced on the tank. No cap, no helmet, the carefully cultivated curl at the front of my 'Tony Curtis' losing its spring in the blow-back.

After a few months of acclimatisation and just a few grazed knees and elbows I got a bit ambitious and decided to test myself on the open road. I planned a trip down to Palmerston North, 102 miles from Hastings, just beyond the southern reach of the Hawke's Bay border. Why Palmerston North? Aunty Betty and Uncle Les Arnett, two close friends of Mum and Dad's, had recently moved there. Les was an old Merchant Navy mate of Dad's and Betty was a large and loud Scottish lassie with insistent claims to a level of society much higher than her actual position. This constant climbing had reduced Les to a position of humble servitude slightly to the left of and behind her impressive bosom. I could never imagine this quiet, timid man being a close buddy of Dad's back in those days of hair-raising Pacific convoys and all-out shore leave roistering.

But there they were, Betty and Les, always up for a hearty party in their big house on Napier Hill. Whenever we stayed, my sisters and I would lie quietly in the dark under the covers of the master bed listening to their musical comedy friend gargle his way through 'Cottage By the Lee'. We wouldn't doze off until we'd heard it at least once.

Les had been offered a good job as chief engineer at the Glaxo factory just out of Palmerston North in the little satellite village of Bunnythorpe. While Dad kept the compressors pumping in his great mutton-reeking pile, Les drifted about in a hairnet among his shiny vats of milk powder.

So, off I went, girding my loins with my independently legged oilskin chaps; breakdown kit and pyjamas in my saddle bags and my Second World War fighter pilot's leather helmet and goggles, courtesy of Stiffy Merton, pulled tight over my head. Biggles on a bike. No visor, no windscreen, not much of anything really, just me and my oilskins and freezing works leather mittens foolishly choosing to head off into a southerly rainstorm on a very long road.

It wasn't too bad at first, and I soldiered on until I hit the seemingly endless Takapau Plains where, unimpeded by any hill or dale, the rain became horizontal. The push-back proved to be a bit too much for my 175ccs and somewhere in the middle of this featureless landscape the chain jumped its sprocket with a heart-sinking graunch and I drifted to a standstill. This wasn't usually a biggie, but brought to a halt this far from any visible civilisation and standing there like a dummy in my armour-like oilskins, quietly contemplating the vinyl saddle pooling with water and the chain hanging sadly from the rear hub, I seriously began to question the wisdom of my odyssey. But I pulled myself together, levered the chain back into line, mopped the seat, kicked over the Villiers and was on my way again, puttering off triumphantly towards Bunnythorpe and Betty and Les's company home.

Aunty Betty greeted me at the door with her usual enthusiastic Scottish hooting and welcomed me inside. What a strange, quiet house. After our great clanking barn of a place, where every surface and service — floorboards, wooden table and chairs (the ubiquitous

Polish bentwoods), biscuit tins, the coal range, back screen door and the cast-iron toilet cistern — made a racket, stepping into Glaxo mansions was like stepping into a deprivation chamber.

But after peeling off my unyielding waterproofing under the pitiful front door awning and draping it over the cooling Velocette, step in I did. Even without my bulky outer shell I felt like a burglar shuffling up the Bremworthed hall. Aunt Betty showed me to the guest room, with its impossibly flouncy bed. When I asked her where the toilet was she directed me to a sort of conservatory down at the back of the house where the washhouse (no one called them laundries then) and the toilet shared the sunniest spot in the house (nobody thought anything of that back then either).

As I used the toilet as quietly as I could, I couldn't help noticing, on a doily in front of me on the cistern, a saucer of dead matches next to a box of matches, and no candle in evidence. I asked Dad about it when I got home, and he said it was so Uncle Les could burn off the poo pong after he'd used the toilet. It wasn't the idea that a lit match could achieve this that intrigued me so much as the idea that Les would even leave a smell.

I crept back to the kitchen table. More softness: tablecloth on a tablecloth and cork placemats. Were we going to eat with wooden utensils? As Uncle Les, seated at the head of the table, stuttered through the usual 'And how's school, Richard?' questions, I sat there and stared, thinking what an unusual-looking man he was. He had one of those aquiline, Mr Punch faces: long nose sliding down in a continuous line from his forehead on its way to meeting his chin, which shone as if he'd just polished it with a rag. Huge dark eyebrows crouched on either side of the nasal slide like clumps of tussock arching out over an eroded riverbank.

Aunty Betty served up corned beef and white sauce with — a new one on me — cauliflower cheese. A polite and creamy meal that went perfectly with the general décor. Then bedtime. Frills right around the edge of the pillow case and lots of feathers in the eiderdown. Please, God, keep all my dreams dry tonight, I prayed, as I drifted off to sleep in the dappled light of the ruched curtains.

Porridge for breakfast — very Scottish and nothing weird there — but Aunty Betty also offered me some toast and marmalade. This immediately took me back to my brush with marmalade at the Hastings hospital, which then took me back to a strange conversation I'd heard from the back seat of the Austin as we'd driven back from one of our visits to Betty and Les. Mum told us that Aunty Betty had had a 'lady's operation' and they'd taken out a lot of her insides. Quite sensibly, I thought, I asked what they'd put in the resulting space, and Dad said, 'Sawdust.' By the time I was old enough to get my motorbike licence I knew this was nonsense, but I could never look at her without thinking of all that loose packing. And I must have been looking at her like that now.

Aunty Betty favoured cat's-eye spectacles, perched above an impressive, spongy Roman nose, which loomed, in turn, large over a wide, red mouth. Her heavy Scottish face definitely demanded attention, and right now it was demanding mine. Undeterred by the Frizzell death stare, she announced that she had a surprise for me. Well, I was going to be the first one to see it.

She sailed regally to the door, Les stood and followed serenely, as usual, and I rose and trailed after them — out the front door, past the Velocette and around to the gravel forecourt in front of the garage. Parked there was a very large black car.

'This,' said Aunty Betty, gesturing like a conjurer, 'is a Bentley!'

And not just any Bentley apparently, but a very *special* Bentley.

Still making the conjuring flourishes, Betty opened the driver's door and beckoned me forward, all the while pointing to the base of the doorframe. I stepped up obediently and there, right in the middle of the frame, and only visible when the door was open, was a small plaque with the number '5' engraved in it.

'*This*,' she cried again, relishing the moment, even if it was rather wasted on this bewildered 15-year-old, 'is one of the cars chosen to accompany the Queen on her visit to New Zealand in 1953. And this car was the fifth in line in the procession!'

Oh my!

I think I'd forgotten about Betty's big moment by the time I blatted through Waipukurau on my way home. All I could remember to tell Mum and Dad was the story of the matches in the toilet.

The author's high school drawing
of Frankenstein's monster.

28

FRANKENSTEIN IS NOT THE MONSTER

Who remembers the first movie they saw? I've been asking around but most people respond with the first movie they *remember* seeing. It's not a trustworthy research method.

The first movies I would've seen must have been those black and white Castle films shown on that flatbed truck out at the Te Awanga camping ground. And I guess my first actual cinema experience would have been at the Embassy, the bughouse, up at the far end of town. It was not necessarily the poor end of town, but commerce definitely took a bit of a dive up there — musty hole-in-the-wall shops half-filled with peculiarly indifferent articles.

The Embassy specialised in serialisation: lots of cowboy movies with classic cliffhanger endings. The portly theatre manager, stuffed into an important-looking suit, would strut out onstage, stand in front of the curtain and give us a bit of a preamble, which was nice of him but somewhat surplus to requirements, considering the febrile atmosphere in the dimly lit hall.

We all knew that the endings were a cop-out. On one Saturday the blazing wagon would hurtle over the cliff with the hero tugging frantically on the reins as the whole rig, with those weirdly backwards spinning wheel-spokes, plunged to its doom. The following Saturday the same blazing wagon would launch out into the void, just as our hero appeared through the smoke and flames, leaping to safety. Did they seriously think we'd be taken in by this pathetic ruse? Well, we seemed to be. Every week. I think we came to accept it as part of the drama, and who cared anyway, as long as the thing kept moving. Action meant action, whatever form it took. Just keep propelling it across the screen and we were happy.

And 'propelled' is definitely the appropriate description here. They always seemed to be galloping past the same bit of scenery. Anything vaguely like a close-up, for which the shoot had to be controlled to some extent, meant a studio set-up where the background would be scrolled along behind the actors as they sat there pretending to be riding horses in front of it. After a while you'd be thinking, 'Haven't I seen that bush before? And those rocks?'

After an hour or so of this we'd rush from the theatre, leap onto our pushbikes and gallop them up the main street, tugging the handlebars upwards, balancing on the back wheel and waving our free hand in the air. 'Yahoo!' Those filmmakers knew their audience.

Occasionally, management would give away wonderful black

and white head shots of the current hero: Tom Mix, Gene Autry, Kit Carson, Hopalong Cassidy, Roy Rogers. Try those names for size. Brad Pitt — really?

Tom Mix, what was he about, with his towering white dome of a stetson, his weirdly groomed eyebrows, his slicked down curls and his smooth Greek snout? I wonder where those pictures, with the signature printed at a jaunty 45-degree angle in the bottom right-hand corner, are now. Imagine how many of them the studios would have had to print for one of them to have made it to my bedroom wall in Hastings.

Another odd thing I had to learn to deal with on those heady cinema mornings was an actor popping up as a different character, after being killed in his last appearance. I remember the first time it happened. A tall, tanned American actor called, as I later found out, Jeff Chandler, made a career out of pretending to be various 'Indian' chiefs. He'd be summarily dispatched in one movie, only to re-emerge with a different wig in a subsequent movie a few weeks later. The cowboy heroes never died, of course, so there was no problem there: Gene Autry was always going to be Gene Autry, no matter what he did.

And then there was the event that brought the town to a standstill, the Movie Marathon: all-day movies, back to back, no intervals. You could arrive in the middle of a movie, watch it to the end, sit through a completely different film and, with any luck, catch the beginning of the film you walked in on. I loved spotting the join when you got to the bit that linked the two halves.

Most of the films were crazy collages of incoherent action anyway, like those Tarzan movies that leapt from location to location without any fear of continuity. Tarzan would be up in the crown of a very artificial-looking tree, gazing intently out over location footage of untrammelled savannah receding into the gauzy distance. Nothing ever matched: he'd be swimming furiously in a fake studio pool, followed by more spotty location footage of hundreds of crocodiles putzing around on a muddy riverbank. The things we put up with, hardly batting an eye in case we missed something.

Oddly, I seemed to grow up in step with the movies. By the time some of the greatest hits turned up I was old enough to take them on board. The first of these blockbusters that I remember was a mad Technicolor romp called *Genevieve*, a frothy British comedy about two shiny vintage cars racing each other across a very picturesque England. The 'bad' car was a huge, yellow bearcat of a thing with miles of exhaust pipes snaking out from under its endless bonnet, and the challenger was a cute little red and black ooga-ooga motorised buggy, the classic image of a 'vintage' car. This was the one we were all meant to root for, and it was called, of course, Genevieve.

I loved the movie, saw it six times. I fell in love with the girlfriend of the bully boy driving the roaring monster and possibly kept going back just for her. The actress's name was Kay Kendall and she stole my heart. Near the end of the movie, when the bad car had been beaten, and they were all celebrating in a swanky nightclub, a tipsy Kay lurched to her feet, swayed over to the stage and demanded that one of the trumpet players relinquish his instrument and give it to her, as she memorably said, 'I'll show them how to tray the plumpet!' And blow me down, she did — well, Kenny Baker did. But she seemed to blow it like nobody's business, and not one smear of her bright red lipstick was dislodged from those luscious lips.

The other big hit, a couple of years later, was the British film *Geordie* about a simple Highland lad, a very *large* simple Highland lad, who came from his humble Scottish village to win the hammer throw at the 1956 Olympic Games. Man, they wrung the juice out of that one. His bonnie wee lass calls out at a strategic moment, and after much adversity, 'Come away, ma wee Geordie', and he wins. Oh, my beating heart.

One of my weirdest movie experiences was going off to the relatively posh State cinema with Dad to watch a bloodthirsty yarn called *King of the Khyber Rifles*. I'm not sure what sparked this great act of fathering. I suspect he really wanted to see the movie and doing so on his own would've been unprecedented, so along I went.

The movie was the sort of example of derring-do that connected Dad to his favourite *Boy's Own Paper*: stories of conquering colonisation up in the great gorges of the Hindu Kush, exhausted soldiers prone behind their butchered horses as they calmly loaded their Webley revolvers, readying themselves for the final assault. What a film. CinemaScope and Technicolor — a *lot* of Technicolor: bright red coats and blood-red blood.

One unforgettable scene featured a hostage sent back as a message to the British — sent back dead, strapped to his horse, lying face down across the saddle, the blood from a serious head wound dripping down the animal's neck. I looked across at Dad, which was weird in itself, having him sitting there right next to me staring straight ahead like a complete stranger. I think he'd forgotten that I was even there. It was a defining moment.

Which brings me to the other defining moment, the first Hammer Film Productions Frankenstein movie, *The Curse of Frankenstein.* I was 14, old enough for an R13, and almost wishing I was 12 again. This was an extremely horrific movie. The old black and white Boris Karloff version had its moments, but looked a bit stiff and cartoonish even to our uneducated eyes. This production was another level of authentic altogether. The creature really did look as if he was stitched together with bits from different corpses — no bolt in the neck. The bath thing he was nurtured in rendered all the skin like wrinkled tripe, white and bloodless, the gut stitching barely containing the tattered fringes of rotting flesh, the two eyeballs floating in the large specimen jar, glaring out balefully from their stringy halo of albumen.

Peter Cushing was utterly convincing as the demented doctor, Christopher Lee as the monster. I was totally persuaded that the experiment was entirely possible. Connect the whole thing up, drop a decent brain in there and then zap it into life. What could possibly go wrong? I can't remember; I was too far gone from the moment of resuscitation to take any more in.

But I do remember walking home in the dark. After I'd said goodbye to Ian Brigham on the corner of Heretaunga Street and Riverslea Road, I had to negotiate the last few blocks across to 507 on my own. The hedges and fences on either side of me became incredibly threatening and I took to the middle of the road, slowly quickening the pace until I was running down the dotted line like a boy possessed. I came to our drive-through by the boxthorn hedge and pounded up the last stretch, under the even darker walnut tree and past the big shed, gasping like a line-caught gurnard.

Just as I went to swerve up the concrete path that led from

the driveway to the back verandah, a disembodied head appeared before me, hanging in space like a wreath of cigarette smoke. I let out a shriek, flung my arms out in front of me and lunged towards the back steps. Then another one appeared and splashed into my eye. They were sweat droplets on my eyelashes, fear-of-Frankenstein's-monster sweat. The first droplet must've caught a flare from the porch light as I turned for home.

I staggered into the kitchen and plonked down in the cane chair next to Dad, who was dozing in front of the coal range, stared at the flames in the grate and decided I might keep that little apparition all to myself.

Johnny Devlin, performing
with the Devils circa 1956.

29

MILKSHAKES WITH THE DEVIL

Was Johnny Devlin even his real name? Johnny yes, but Devlin? With its barely concealed rock'n'roll satanic message? Impossible, but true. Born in Raetihi into a family of Country and Western musicians who conveniently called themselves The Devlin Family, Johnny got his first guitar on his eleventh birthday, and joined the band. Mum and Dad eventually quit and the boys carried on as The River City Ramblers, courtesy of Whanganui, the river city they'd long ago graduated to. Possibly due to the pressure of Johnny's rampant ambition, the brothers then faded from the scene and Johnny continued as a solo act, yodelling round the local talent quest circuit. Until he heard Elvis Presley singing 'Heartbreak Hotel'.

I knew that moment: I heard it myself, in Hastings. Probably on the same broadcast. What a song — all that echo, hiccupping phrasing and quivering passion. It was like a portal to a place where no parents, teachers, prefects or piano teachers could go. And Johnny Devlin, born with a rock'n'roll name, felt it too, and pretty much decided on the spot that he was going to be New Zealand's Elvis Presley.

Somehow he miraculously made his way up to Auckland and word spread. A sly old fox called Phil Warren did a Colonel Parker and set Johnny up with a band put together from a canny selection of top Auckland musicians who went on to become The Devils. Their first single, an obscure Elvis Presley B-side called 'Lawdy Miss Clawdy', went ballistic: it sold 10,000, huge numbers in New Zealand in those days. Screaming girls waited outside the theatres for the chance to rip the loosely (surely) stitched sleeves from Johnny's sweaty shirts.

By the time he hit the Embassy in Hastings he was in full hip-swing. Compared with his manic performance, the support act, the Howard Morrison Quartet, came across as a musical comedy turn. What a concert. That chubby little Raetihi cherub, with his oily frizz hammered into a passable Tony Curtis and his well-rehearsed rock'n'roll moves, *was* New Zealand's Elvis Presley. Of that there could be no doubt.

The next day, Saturday, Philip Morris and I went out for a milkshake with him in Napier. How did that happen? He must have been staying at Phil's father's hotel in Hastings. I can't think of any other plausible reason why the two of us would be squiring Johnny Devlin round Hawke's Bay on a sunny Saturday, but there we were, with a motley selection of try-hard bodgies and widgies, crowding a couple of booths in an Emerson Street milkbar.

Somehow, down here in New Zealand, we never quite got the memo about the rebel clothing protocols and our bodgies and teddy boys tended to blur back and forth from camp to gangster with impressive dexterity. The Māori boys from the Tomoana Freezing Works dormitories had the teddy boy thing covered in all manner of original and creative ways. I don't how they did it. Eli Morris, a giant and scary-looking softie, somehow managed to cobble together enormous drape coats in black satin with leopard-skin collars, held together with a single button somewhere down at knee level. Actually, not a button but a small gold chain, with a gold button at either end, like a flash cufflink. Who made that for him? He certainly didn't buy it off the rack at Poppelwells. Underneath this wonderful waterfall of an arrangement he wore a lilac shirt anchored at the throat with a black string tie. The entire ensemble tapered down to peg-leg trousers and colossal crepe-soled brothel creepers. One of the Jacobs boys from the sawmill round the corner from me managed a similar draped look, but Eli took the prize.

I go into some detail here because these outfits fascinated me and I would spend a serious amount of school time designing outfits along similar lines in the back of my exercise books. In real life all I could manage was a modest white-boy look with my carefully cultivated flat-top and a reversible windcheater like the one Sal Mineo wore in *Rebel Without a Cause*: red and black panels on one side and black with black and white houndstooth panels on the other. Definitely bought from Poppelwells. On the occasion under discussion I would've been wearing the black and white side over a white T-shirt, black jeans, white socks and my sturdy oxbloods. And Philip, elegantly cool as usual in whatever he chose to climb into, pretending he hadn't given his attire a second thought.

We even had a local bikie gang — all two of them — the leader of the pack and his sidekick. The LOTP had the mysterious demeanour of a professional criminal. He looked like a young, uncreased Grant Dalton with a grim mouth and a scruffy crewcut, always squinting off into the distance as if he was constantly looking for where he should have been. His sidekick was a bleached-haired psychopath who, it was rumoured, had thrown a patron out of the closed window of Paxi's pool hall.

Components of this meagre talent pool of rock'n'roll fans composed the merry band toasting Johnny Devlin with malted milkshakes in a Napier milkbar. Then the world's two most organic and feral bodgies — Slats and Darcy, the two noisiest guys in the Bay — ambled in and joined the party. Darcy, I suspect, was in his usual Tomoana Freezing Works-issue clothing, boots and all. Slats would've been in his long, drain-pipe jeans and a greasy little leather jerkin he'd picked up somewhere. Neither boy dressed to impress. I doubt they even knew what a bodgie was.

After the initial drawn breath and awkward silence, Eli leant in and said, 'Are — you going — to — play — that — Al-fiss Press-ley — song — about — the — ho*tel*?'

Slats bellowed, 'Do you know that crazy bastard John Chadwick? He's from Raetihi.' Darcy, who always took his cue from his older brother, echoed, in full cry, 'Yeah, Raetihi!'

Philip asked Johnny what it was like touring — all the girls and so on. Johnny said it was crazy, man, crazy, but starting to get a bit boring. Not a great conversationalist, our Johnny, just sitting there in the corner of the booth, taking it all in. Like me.

Then there was a huge roar of motorcycle noise, the loud click and clack of kick-stands and the bikie gang in their squeaky leather armour clumped in. The already-nervous staff who were bunched at the rear of the premises cracked at the arrival of these two bandits and the manager came over and asked us to leave.

And here's the great bit, Johnny Devlin, *the* Johnny Devlin, was lounging and grinning, very relaxed, beneath a poster announcing the Napier concert that night that featured a large black and white portrait of our boy. Despite the weight of empirical evidence, the manager continued to froth and foam, screaming, '*Out!*' and pointing to the door with a quivering finger.

I was happy to go. I was starting to quiver a bit myself, especially at the sight of the bikie duo stirring in their seats, but Johnny looked pretty ensconced, and Slats and Darcy weren't going anywhere. Then the police were called, and we went — up to Marine Parade, where we congregated defiantly in the curved gazebo thing by the soundshell. Grog appeared from somewhere, whereupon the vigilant police force reappeared and banished us to beyond the city limits. We were kicked out of Napier. I was pretty impressed.

Slats and company decided to set up camp right there, on the beach, a yard outside the 30 mph sign. Mr Devlin and his entourage had decamped by this point and even my adventurous friend Philip was starting to have second thoughts. I was on about my third or fourth.

The assembled rabble's cars and motorbikes magically appeared at the gravel's edge, car boots were opened and refreshments were served. Night had fallen and a large driftwood bonfire, petrol driven no doubt, suddenly flared up on the stony beach. At this point Phil and I showed our adventurous mettle and sneaked off into the night, back to Phil's dad's Plymouth. The last thing I remember as we disappeared down a convenient side street was Slats silhouetted at the edge of the fire with a crate of a dozen big brown bottles dangling from the end of a very long arm as he kicked a flaming log into the sky while cheerfully giving two great knuckly fingers to the police watching from the safety of Napier city.

Phil and I went home. Johnny went to Australia and in 2008 was made a Member of the New Zealand Order of Merit.

Being a teenager had hardly been invented; we all just strayed into it, making it up as we went along. Listening to Little Richard in the special listening booths at the back of Begg's music store on a Friday night, catching the Lever Hit Parade on the Mantle radio in the living room. I don't think any of us thought we were missing out on much. And we had a local singing sensation, one of the Bennett brothers from the pā out at Fernhill, who sang down at the Trades Hall where the Māori girls danced in formation with their purses down on the floor at their shuffling feet. We thought we were pretty flash. You could buy jeans and 'flecked' sports coats at Poppelwells, just a few doors down from Aunty Molly's dress shop. And if you couldn't buy it, you made it up. Took one of your dad's old 'thousand acre jackets', turned the lapels up and cut off two of the three buttons.

This new rock'n'roll thing wasn't allowed at school dances but we managed to sneak it in with an out-of-control interpretation of a peculiarly aggressive, but permissible, dance called 'Ballin' the Jack'. We had no real idea of what we were doing, but we had a hell of a lot of fun. The new Zephyr Zodiac was on display in the middle of the shiny floor of the Ford dealership, and another new sensation came to town: the Twist. An enterprising couple taught the dance to packed halls up and down the country. I got pretty good at it.

Hastings Boys' High School.

30

WHERE'S THE BRICK?

We all knew it from the street, its exotic façade hunkered back in the conifers just up the road from the intermediate school, but cycling right up to the impressive Cape Dutch-style main building and then continuing past it into the vast mystery of the actual high school was an awe-inspiring revelation. Everything looked so grown-up. Even the bike sheds were intimidating. They reminded me of the covered cattle yards at the A&P show, stretching off into the distance with all the bikes lined up in the gloaming like patient livestock. What were the rules? Where did you park your bike?

The actual school buildings themselves were even more overwhelming. Large, old-fashioned brick barrack-like structures arranged at right angles to the rear of the administration block like tables at a wedding reception. If it wasn't for the white pebble-dash finish of the welcoming portico and those decorative cypresses I could have been back in one of my POW novels.

The outside assembly area was a narrow quadrangle of marked-out concrete between the assembly hall and the number one classroom block. The dark buildings looming over the space also lent a claustrophobic effect to the morning gathering. Being herded into this canyon with several hundred other boys all clad in various shades of navy blue serge certainly served to remind you that you were there for some serious schooling.

It was always a relief to get the command to file into the hall and sit down, though this feeling was short-lived because we then had to sit through assembly. The end of this exercise in numbing boredom was always signalled by music. It had obviously been decided that for the good of our moral spirit, our musical education and our aural health, we were to get a good solid dose of classical music every morning.

The music master took this responsibility extremely seriously. He would approach the podium like the Archbishop of Canterbury, softly intone with perfect enunciation the order of play for the day, then retreat backwards with head bowed, to his chair, where he would sit, with head still bowed, cross his legs, put one hand, palm down on one trousered thigh, fingers facing forwards, and slowly run the tips of the fingers of the second hand up and down in the grooves between the knuckles of the first. All in an act of extreme concentration.

Some sixth former out the back somewhere would lower the needle down onto the vinyl, rather fearfully I would imagine, as any nervous jitter would come through the PA with an exaggerated graunch — which was always something to look forward to. The music that followed was mostly a complete mystery to us, unless it was the theme from *The Lone Ranger*, which was guaranteed to get us all going. I don't think Mr Pious up on the stage had ever seen the movie serial (no TV in the 1950s) and always seemed mystified by our sudden enthusiasm for that morning's choice.

Our favourite bits were the Bachs or the Beethovens that had the false endings, where several of the masters would gather their gowns around them and get halfway to their feet before the final climax kicked in. Ha, gotcha. You could even, if you were quick enough, see a ghost of a smirk cross the music master's face.

Leaving assembly was the riskiest part of the day for all the fashionistas among us. The vice-principal, Chook Fowler, would stand at the door as we all filed out, drilling us with his X-ray eyes, looking out for a peek of T-shirt, fancy belts (slim and pink), sleeves rolled mid-forearm, shirts untucked and so on. Any flouter of uniform law would be tapped with his rolled-up assembly notes and made to stand to the side round by the motorbike lean-to where we would eventually get the 'buck up your ideas' lecture, again with the rolled up foolscap notes jabbing your chest for emphasis as he tried, in his weird, scary way, to be reasonable.

His forced avuncular beam was marred somewhat by a strange physical anomaly: he had a large flat disc of smooth shiny tissue right in the middle of his forehead, an area of total calm at the centre of all the intense furrows. We couldn't imagine its origin, though we all had ideas, the favourite being a botched lobotomy. But whatever the origin of the blank third eye, it made it very difficult to concentrate on the inspirational message.

Curiously enough, that gap between the admin building and

the assembly hall where, much later, we could, if we were lucky enough to have one, park our motorbikes, was very visible from the assembly area and every morning I could catch a glimpse of my trusty Velocette slotted away in there, which gave me an odd sense of mastery over the occasion.

But that's a long way from my first day at high school, nervously cowering somewhere at the indifferent end of the great crowd of boys, wondering when I might be mobbed and have the knob on the top of my cap torn off. For this was the ritual, apparently: some sort of initiation ceremony where a self-elected gang of boisterous seniors would corner you in the toilets and render you knobless. (My sad double-entendre, not theirs.) Some new boys mutilated their own caps to avoid the confrontation.

For some dim reason I thought they'd never notice me, but they did. I stood there with my back to the urinal, handed the cap over and watched as some feverish wally tore the knob off with his teeth. He could've eaten the whole cap for all I cared. I hated the stupid-looking thing and took special exception to wearing it because of that issue of the irritating crease across the carefully cultivated crewcut.

'Accidents' constantly befell the wretched cap. 'Blew off my head and landed in a puddle!' was a favourite riposte until it started to wear a bit thin with the monitors, especially on windless days. You could keep it folded, military style, in your belt and risk detention, which didn't seem to be too high a price to pay for a crease-free flat-top. I didn't really mind detention, which sounded worse than it was: half an hour or so after school in the hall with all the other outlaws. I once memorised, under orders, one of Mark Antony's biggest speeches from *Julius Caesar* and could quote it for years, standing on the kitchen table at parties.

'Socks up!' was another command the authorities soon got sick of issuing if you were determined enough. God, that bloody uniform. Funny how it could look so different on so many different boys. Every individual had ways, conscious or otherwise, of customising the exact same set of clothing to their various personalities.

And then, speaking of uniforms, there was military training, or barracks, as it was sometimes called. Some teachers, and some senior boys, took it *very* seriously, barking and strutting like something out of a movie. But some of us couldn't grasp the seriousness of the concept at all.

The platoon I ended up in seemed to be made up almost entirely of miscreants. I don't know if we were specially selected and clumped together for easy management, but it worked. We kind of went along with all the parade ground stuff, almost all of us marching in order, and we got the drill more or less right but we never quite *looked* right. An ambiguous aura of disarray hung over us like the dirt cloud around that character in the *Peanuts* comic strip. It was hard for the platoon sergeant to put his finger on but he knew something was awry. On the day that the governor-general came to the school to inspect the troops, our platoon was shut up in the library for the duration.

I know what it was. It was the uniforms. There were a sizeable number of Māori boys in the motley line-up and their liberties with the uniform were uncanny: mixing and mismatching, tucking in or not tucking in, sleeveless pullovers 'pulled over' over the entire jacket somehow.

There were twin boys who never took their uniforms home but kept them stuffed into their desks, whether by design or not, I don't know. But on barracks day they would fish these mangled balls of khaki out of their confinement and climb into them, as is. They looked as if they'd been bull-whipped and dragged behind a galloping horse, yet when they stood proudly at attention among the rest of us they almost looked OK. I think it was the consistency of the sartorial shambles that somehow allowed us to get away with it.

I wore oxblood shoes with enormous crepe soles and had cultivated enough verdigris on my buttons and badge as to render them almost black. Ah, those oxblood shoes. They sported a lovely sort of plaited upper on a level plain between the toe and the big floppy laces. And I mean really plaited — not that lazy loafer basket weave. One day, when we were out aerating the cricket pitch, armed with a variety of manure forks, potato forks and pitchforks and jabbing away at the grass, I managed to drive my fork down through the oxblood plaiting, through the big toe just to the left of the nail and into the leather sole. I needed the help of Big Gavin to get it out. I could see blood bubbling up through the decorative plaiting — my blood with oxblood. I hoped that if I left the shoe on it'd act as a sort of bandage. It didn't.

I wasn't the only one to put his foot in it. A strange Scottish boy in the group managed to drive his broad-bladed potato fork right through his shoe, through the arch of his foot and into the ground with incredible force. Perhaps he was angry at being dragooned into such a menial task. He took his hands off the fork handle, leaving it slowly waving back and forth, and cried out, 'That's my best pair of shoes. Mum is going to kill me!'

But what lovely grounds we had. Because Hastings Boys' was out on the edge of town, it was hard to see where school stopped and the countryside began. This served us well during the dreaded marathon. Off would go the pack, all elbows and white singlets, puffing off up towards the Pakipaki limeworks. Not far from the school, where we started to get into the rough and the cluster was starting to stretch out a bit, I saw one of the Māori boys slope off casually into the long grass on the side of the road. I stopped for one of those fake breathers — hands on hips, trunk bent slightly forward — and ducked in after him. I got there in time to see him crawling into a large culvert that went back underneath the road we'd just been on.

As was usual with him, he wasn't the slightest bit surprised to see me, quickly followed by Gavin, then Simon and Leo. We sat huddled in the big concrete pipe, feeling very pleased with ourselves, until the pack started dribbling back overhead, at which point we subtly blended back into the wheezing multitude and crossed the line like champions.

What a strange, guileless little fellow Wharepapa was. Short and skinny with a huge shock of orangey brown hair that seemed to attract all manner of debris — straw, leaves, small sticks — he was the go-to guy I enlisted way back in primary school when I decided to change my name from the limp, goody-goody Richard to the more manly and exciting Dick. I asked him to call the new name out loud from the other side of the classroom so that everyone would turn to see who the appellation was directed at. He went to it in his usual wide-eyed way, and it worked. By the time I got to intermediate, everyone outside the family was calling me Dick.

Incredibly resourceful, but with no obvious objective awareness of it, he seemed to think his lateral view of the world was completely normal and that there was nothing unique or unusual about his unmediated observations. I was standing next to him in the playground one day, over by the plane trees where I'd fought the Havelock bus crew at the beginning of the year, watching a noisy crowd of boys pushing and shoving around a curious disturbance in the centre of the ruck, when the scariest teacher in the school strolled up and said, 'What's going on here?' It obviously wasn't a fight as there was no hole in the middle of the melee, just an indeterminate focal point.

My friend looked up at the teacher, eyes wide with excitement, and replied enthusiastically, 'Waterhouse has some rude pictures, sir.' I was amazed. He wasn't saying it in a dobbing-in sort of way; he just seemed to think that the master would be genuinely interested. Waterhouse seemed to have an inexhaustible supply of rude pictures: saucy postcards and those crude little line-drawing comic books with their eye-popping cartoon pornography. He must've found his father's stash. They lived on the eastern outskirts of town, on the orchard where we used to stage our limestone-loaded air rifle wars. The whole domestic scene out there exuded a weird Ozarkian frisson, including the flirty older sister with her long freckled legs and her flimsy coal-miner's daughter frocks.

We did have some great teachers, though, down in the ghetto of the lower professional classes, particularly our French teacher, who was German. He had such a reckless scholastic manner that we couldn't wait to see what he would do next. He told obscure bawdy jokes: 'Did you hear about the swan chasing around after all the cygnet (signet) rings?' Maybe it was designed to teach us about the ambiguity of language. He was also a demon chalk chucker. With his back to us as he wrote out prepositions on the blackboard, he seemed to be able to figure out who was doing all the muttering behind him and he'd suddenly spin about, knitted tie and tweed jacket flying, and hurl the chalk with alarming accuracy at the chatterer. It was nearly always Wharepapa so he was mostly on target.

Whare was one of his favourites, funnily enough, because he seemed to be able to speak perfect French. He never knew what he was saying, but he said it perfectly. Actually, most of the Māori boys in the class were able to do this. Must have been the cadence or something. The real favourite was a tall, quietly spoken fellow named Nana Kamau, who the teacher frequently called upon to speak. He would stand and hold forth from the textbook while the teacher sat at his desk with his chin propped on one hand listening dreamily while sucking on another Capstan plain. I got pretty good at all the 'la plume de ma tante' stuff, but was always too nervous to attempt it out loud.

The twins were in the French class too, but, it sometimes seemed, only one at a time. The teacher reckoned they had only one school uniform and had to share it. He was always sending boys over to his house, just down the road, for cigarettes and tobacco mostly, and one day one of the biggest boys in the class came back and breathlessly informed us that the teacher's wife had come to the door in a nightie and a 'loosely fastened' dressing gown.

This pitched all our teenage imaginations into overdrive. Some of the more adventurous would even ask our teacher if there was anything he needed from home. Simon, I think, actually got to go on one of these errands and he reported that the wife just opened the door, fully dressed, and handed the tobacco over with a sigh before going back inside.

Kind and gentle Nana. I got quite close to him in the course of the fifth form year and one day he took me out to Bridge Pā, where he lived. In contrast to his shy and retiring nature, Nana occasionally appeared on the biggest motorbike in the school. He sounded like 10 motorcyclists thundering up the drive. It was a Triumph, probably a 650, and it made my Velocette look like a toy. Anyway, on this particular day, Nana had to go back home for something and he invited me along. He got me to climb up behind him on the pillion seat and he told me to hang on tight. And off we roared, up the long straights between orchards all the way out to Bridge Pā.

This was a new experience for me. Houses, sheds, cars, trucks dotted about everywhere — no fences or apparent borders — except a graveyard, which was fenced, as were some of the graves inside. Nana drove up to one of the old weatherboard houses and we went in down the hall, past lots of framed photos of old Māori people. Room after room with nothing but piles of mattresses in them. My eyes were swivelling like a gecko's. The kitchen–living room was full of uncles and aunties sitting on couches and armchairs covered with colourful peggy-square blankets and cushions and there was food all over the table. (Maybe I'd turned up at morning tea.) The walls were covered in a collage of framed portraits, samplers and calendar landscapes, pictures of the Queen and many more family portraits hung almost to the ceiling. I don't remember Nana having a room of his own like mine at 507: every space just seemed to flow into the next.

It had been a new experience for me, the skinny white kid, and I thought a lot about that on the way back to school as we blatted down those poplar-lined avenues. Until my reverie was interrupted by Nana taking it upon himself to lean forward over the petrol tank in some random need for speed, thereby letting the full force of the wind hit me directly in the chest, bending me way backwards over the rear mudguard. If it hadn't been for my bulky oxbloods catching beneath Nana's large crepe-soled desert boots I might still be bouncing down Riverslea Road.

Another French teacher, a more senior one, couldn't have been more of a contrast to our boisterous German. He was a short, mousy little fellow, with a wild white Einstein haircut, who seemed to be inordinately attached to his gown. He wore it everywhere, and it was almost totally wrecked. It trailed out in ribbons behind him as he walked across the quad, as if he'd just escaped a mauling by a pack of rabid chihuahuas. Maybe it was a badge-of-honour thing, the ancient order of the gown, slowly going a mossy green across the shoulders as it decayed from the hem up.

Our science teacher was an interesting fellow: a spritely little silent movie-looking character someone had nicknamed Honk because he walked with an odd, sprightly bounce, both eyebrows raised as if every step he made surprised him, as if his shoes honked and he could never figure out where the sound was coming from. Wiry body, wiry hair. He bounced his shoulders, too, when he spoke, elbows clamped to his sides — lots of little shrugs with eyebrows working in unison, as if he was letting you in on a private joke. Very generous with his time, he took us for bush walks and loved cranking up the Bunsen burners in class and creating loud, sulphurous explosions. We all rather adored Honk.

So many teachers, not all of them memorable, but here's another one: Fred Benge, a seriously eccentric fellow who loved reminiscing. If you could get him going on something even vaguely related to the subject he could waste half the period telling us all about it.

Someone organised a fantastic stunt in class one day: we were all to slowly edge our desks forward in quiet increments whenever his back was to us — it took him forever to get his message onto the blackboard — stopping as soon as he turned back to the class. The seats and desks were attached by runners, like sledges, which meant you could shuffle them forward with your feet on the ground, like motorvating a dysfunctional pedal car. Fred couldn't figure it out. When he turned for the final time, the boys at the front row were almost at his feet. I remember him looking down at us, all innocent, as he scratched his bristly old grey crewcut. We stayed like that till the end of class and shuffled them all back later.

Our history teacher seemed to be totally over both his subject and teaching. He would slyly read from an open book strategically positioned on a desk by his thigh as he stood before the class, always making sure to keep one or two pages ahead of us. The Bridge Pā boys and the Havelock North bus brigade (brigands) formed a dense mass at the back of his classes that exuded a rather obvious aura of complete lack of interest. I rather liked history, so would position myself strategically somewhere relatively neutral in the ranking: close enough to follow the flow of history, and close enough to the glowering phalanx of mutineers to follow the plotting.

I have very strong memories of Mr Frykberg's physics class, largely because I couldn't follow a word of it (though I'm mad on it now, strangely enough). At the end of one class, 'Fryk' set a list of equations for homework: we were to work on them overnight and we'd be quizzed on them the following day. The dreaded lesson duly arrived and we all sat there waiting. He singled me out: 'I'll ask Frizzell if he's got them right and if he has I'll take it for granted that the whole class has.' I was flattered, and even answered them. It took me a couple of weeks to smell a rat.

I had a strange way of looking at the world — always there, but not quite there, somehow. Somewhere in a neutral sort of middle. In my fourth year I got bottom of the professional one stream, so the next year I was demoted to professional two, where I came top (thanks to art and English). Perfect streaming: I thought it was completely logical.

I thought me and art was completely logical too. 'Where's Frizzell?' 'Hiding in the art room, sir.' Hiding from sport mostly and from PE. Those enormously fat climbing ropes, and that horse thing you had to leapfrog over. I'd run up to it, trying to look as determined as possible, bang both hands at the beginning of the long brown, padded bit, do a little jump in the air, then walk around it looking very disappointed with myself, as if I'd mistimed a perfect 10. And rugby, what a trial. Because I was biggish it was decided that I should be a prop. I would plod around the paddock in a loose jumble of muddy, grunting boys, doing my best to avoid the ball. I touched it once, I think — a weird, greasy, leathery thing.

The only sport that I would admit to was swimming, especially underwater. My mate and I could both do one and a half lengths of the 'Olympic' pool before getting spots before our eyes and great hiccupping chest heaves from the lack of oxygen to our lungs. Always a sign that it might be time to surface.

One of my best underwater stunts was retrieving the brick. I'd figured out that if you exhaled as you went down, you dropped like a stone with just enough in reserve to lie on the bottom of the pool as if you were sunbathing on top of it. On one grand occasion before a full sports-day audience it came time for my big event. Mr Benge was charged with the job of throwing in the brick while I dog-paddled at the edge of the pool in readiness for the big fetch. I'm not sure what happened, but Fred must've thrown a practice dummy or something, because at the first hint of action, down I went. No brick!

So I waited, and waited, and waited, until the chest heaves and eye-spots told me I could wait no more, and swam back to the top. As soon as my head broke the surface, and before I noticed Mr Benge and half the staff kneeling anxiously at the pool's edge peering down into its depths, I called out, very indignantly and clearly, 'Where's the brick?' It became a catchcry at the school for a spell. Apparently Mr Benge had hung onto the brick because he was worried that if he tossed it in while I was down there, it could have landed on my head. And fair enough. We'll never know.

But I do know that eventually all the sports masters and PE teachers got sick of my clowning around and were happy to see me skive off to the art room. A whole room for art! A minor miracle, really, given the general lack of enthusiasm for the subject. This was why it was very easy for me to assume that it was 'my' art room.

But it was very plain to see that it wouldn't be mine until its present owner decamped.

His name was Bryan Dew, a tall and arrogant prodigy who had somehow fenced off the rear of the room in a way that quite emphatically said, 'Do not enter, artist at work.' I used to stand there on the 'public' side of the barrier and gaze in wonderment at the set-up. How had he done it?

When he left — to go on to great things, first in Auckland and then in London — I immediately inserted myself into his domain, only to find it didn't exist. He had somehow dominated the space with a couple of chairs and sheer force of will. All I found was a jumble of furniture and junk that looked pretty much like every other corner of the room. The biggest part of Bryan's skill was simply knowing that he was an artist. He had no doubts about his role whatsoever. I, however, didn't even really know what an artist was. I knew I wanted to be one but had no idea how to go about it. Even now, I still feel like a bit of an imposter.

The art master didn't help. God knows how Bryan managed to cower him, but he obviously did. I, on the other hand, never seemed to be able to make any impression on him of any kind. I knew I was pretty good — I could draw an onion on a brick like nobody's business — but I never received any encouragement.

The art teacher at intermediate, a tall fellow stooped like a cartoon vulture, seemed to enjoy anything I put in front of him. I quickly picked up on his approval sounds — an odd sort of 'sss, sss, sss' issued through a clenched-teeth smile. Once I decided to really put him to the tessst and practised on an image at home: a brightly coloured parrot on its perch. When I had it right I repeated the exercise in class. I think his eyebrows may have gone a bit higher than usual, and the smile a bit wider, but I still only got the same sss, sss, sss.

But it was always going to be more than I got from Mr Williams at high school. Looking back, I wonder if he wasn't a little bit jealous of me, not so much of my nascent ability as my gormless — or innocent — enthusiasm for the subject, and for its positive side. He was convinced that art had to be grim — boils and putrefaction — whereas I was way too much in love with the sunny and the superficial. Too much Batman and not enough Bosch. Story of my life, really.

Even my unbridled fantasies about art school didn't seem to move him and might in fact have irritated the hell out of him. The very picture of the provincial artist/teacher crushed by the local, uncaring peasants, the last thing he would've wanted to hear, or see, was a bright-eyed young fool bouncing round the room like Bugs Bunny raving about art school.

Maybe I'm being too hard on the guy, but I did see a couple of his works at an exhibition in Hastings: dark and subterranean, bronze-green wāhine trapped in a decaying kelp forest, or some such. Even at that tender stage of my art education I did wonder at the tone of the thing.

I must have done something right because I did eventually go on to art school. It took me two goes to get through the School Certificate examination, which slowed things down but didn't bother me unduly; I was enjoying the rhythm of high school. The problem was that, at my first attempt, Mum and Dad wouldn't let me take art.

I've written about this before, about Dad's fear of me ending up a poofter dying in a garret, and how, when challenged, they said I could drop maths for art if I failed. So I failed, deliberately. I wrote 'Merry Christmas' across the opening sheet of the history paper. I almost buggered it up by getting a bit carried away with the English paper, but still managed to fall short of the magic 200.

So I took art. Moved into Bryan Dew's imaginary corner and drew onions on bricks. Painted a green Chianti bottle next to a sliced Vienna and got the reflection of the sliced loaf in the shiny breadknife spot on. Mr Williams failed to be impressed.

Things started to get serious. I applied, and was accepted for, a studentship interview. The politburo eventually turned up, sitting in a row behind a table in the careers adviser's office. The first question they asked me was: 'And tell us, Mr Frizzell, why do you want to be a teacher?' I obviously hadn't read the small print, and shot back straight away, 'Oh, I don't want to be a teacher.' One of the officials mumbled that there was no point in proceeding with the interview, and I found myself back out in the quadrangle wondering whether it was something I'd said. Never mind, I had the freezing works, and Mr Wattie. We'd get by.

School finished in that shambolic, running-down sort of way that ends of years always seem to, though one memorable moment landed like a meteorite in the middle of it. Some time, back in spring, I'd lost the parka-type top of my motorbike wet-weather gear and had reported it to the lost and found department, which also happened to be the senior common room where all we 'grown-up' students would lounge about making toast and drinking Bushells instant coffee. One day I was at home, in my bedroom, when Mum called out from the back of the house, in 'that' voice, and I went to the door to see her confronted by an extremely irate farmer with chapped lips and chilblained ears who was waving my parka at her.

Mum said, 'Do you know anything about this? This gentleman says he found your coat in his barn.' Then the farmer himself burst forth: 'Yes! You lot were having a sex booze-up in my barn and set fire to it! And I have proof that you were there!' I could see then that he had the parka inside out with Mum's carefully sewn name label very much to the fore. By this time I was starting to wish I *had* been there — a sex booze-up in a flaming barn? — but fortunately I had the lost and found report to furnish me with a cast-iron alibi. For a few moments, though, I was definitely there — in the barn, in the parka. Mum kept looking at me sideways for a spell, half-thinking, perhaps, that I'd somehow faked the report.

The countdown to departure day continued. I got caned in the wings of the Municipal Theatre by my old nemesis, Chook Fowler. Had one final pie and gravy down at the Embassy tearooms, and a farewell game of snooker in the billiard hall next door — both 'illegal' activities while in uniform.

At my send-off on the platform of the Hastings railway station a decent crowd of family and friends turned up. Leo tied toilet paper to all the outside appendages of the railcar so that they unrolled and fluttered in the slipstream as the railcar picked up speed and I slowly chugged off south.

Past the Newmans bus depot where I caught the bus to Whakatāne, past Aunty Molly's frock shop where I used to sit in the small tearoom out the back eating biscuits and listening to her talk to her posh clients about hem lengths, past the war memorial library, past Hastings Intermediate where I got clocked with a baseball and came to on the ground saying, 'How many floors did the elevator fall, Mother?', which was one of Jughead's lines from the *Archie* comics, past the hallowed halls of Hastings Boys' High School sitting there among its proud conifers, past the D'Arths' cornfields, past the Pakipaki limeworks, past the pub at Te Aute where Philip Morris's father would drive us so he could have an illegal nip on a Sunday, and on into the wide (cobalt) blue yonder.

ACKNOWLEDGEMENTS

This account of a Hawke's Bay childhood in the 1950s isn't, of course, necessarily mine alone.

I'd like to thank Nicola Legat for pointing this out to me and for helping me to corral a tumbling parade of objectivity and subjectivity. I'd also like to thank Nicola and Anna Rogers for the heroic work they did with my avalanche of ellipses, exclamation marks, capitals and dashes, and with my reckless attempts to understand colons, semi-colons and commas.

And in a last stab at historical accuracy, Anna Jackson-Scott joined the fray and managed to confer some credibility on my more fanciful fictions.

ABOUT THE AUTHOR

Dick Frizzell MNZM is one of New Zealand's best-known painters. He studied at the Ilam School of Fine Arts at the University of Canterbury from 1960 to 1963 and then had a long career in advertising. Alongside his career as a painter, Frizzell is also the highly sought-after designer of a range of products from toys to wine. He is the author of *Dick Frizzell: The painter* (Random House, 2009), *It's All About the Image* (Random House, 2011), *Me, According to the History of Art* (Massey University Press, 2020), *The Sun Is a Star* (Massey University Press, 2021) and *The Dance of the Hooligans* (David Ling Publishing, 2023). Dick exhibits regularly and often works in collaboration with writers and other artists. He lives in Auckland with his wife, Jude.

First published in 2025 by Massey University Press
Private Bag 102904, North Shore Mail Centre
Auckland 0745, New Zealand
www.masseypress.ac.nz

Design: Megan van Staden
Cover photograph of Stiffy Merton and the author: courtesy Dick Frizzell

A catalogue record for this book is available from the National Library of New Zealand

Printed and bound in China by Everbest Investment Ltd

ISBN: 978-1-99-101693-5
eISBN: 978-1-99-101694-2